The Miniature Horse in Review
Volume 1

A Collection of Articles on Miniature Horses

Edited by
Toni M. Leland

Printed in U.S.A.

The Miniature Horse in Review Series
Published by
SMALL HORSE PRESS
a division of Equine Graphics Publishing

537 Drager Street • Ashland, Oregon 97520

Acknowledgments

The Miniature Horse in Review, Volume One is a compilation of in-depth information directed to the Miniature Horse owner, both experienced and novice. The articles on these pages incorporate many ideas and suggestions contributed by Miniature Horse owners, trainers, veterinarians, breeders, and writers in an effort to provide up-to-date relevant information to the Mini enthusiast.

Our thanks to the many sincere contributors to these volumes. We would like to thank the Miniature Horse registries and clubs, which have been extremely helpful with this endeavor, especially the New England Miniature Horse Society and its Public Relations spokeswoman, Cheryl Lekstrom. She has given freely of her time, talent, and photo archives in an effort to make *The Miniature Horse in Review* as complete and attractive as possible. We would also like to thank Roxanne Manderino of Blue Chip Miniatures for her help in tracking down information and verifying data—something we couldn't have done on our own.

©1995 Small Horse Press, a division of Equine Graphics Publishing
All rights reserved. No portion of this publication may be reproduced, transmitted, transcribed, stored in a retrieval system, or translated into any language in any form by any means without written permission of publisher.

First Edition
Library of Congress Card Number: 95-74741
ISBN Number: 1-887932-00-3

The publisher accepts no responsibility for any claims arising from use or application of any information contained in this publication. The material contained herein has been written by outside authors and, while the publisher has made every effort to see that information is true and correct, publisher makes no guarantees, claims, or endorsements of such information. Publisher is not affiliated with any organization or registry, nor any company or individual mentioned in any article, and further denies any endorsement of such organization, registry, or company and/or its policies/products.

Table of Content

The Beginning

History of the Miniature Horse 5
   by Cheryl A. Lekstrom

Section I—Basics of Horse Ownership

Horsekeeping for the Newcomer 13
   by Toni M. Leland
Miniatures in the Backyard: Will Your Zoning Allow It? 21
   by Margaret Anderson-Murphy
Perilous Pasture Plants 24
   by Cindy Fisher
Pedigree & Breeding Terminology 29
   by Susan Larkin
It's 10 oclock-Do You Know Where Your Minis Are? 36
   by Bonnie Kreitler

Section II—Keeping Your Miniature Horse Healthy

Understanding Teeth 43
   by Kenneth L. Marcella, DVM
Basic Foot Structure 49
   by Michael Berluti

Section III—Breeding & Raising Your Own

Reproduction in the Miniature Horse 55
   by Kenneth L. Marcella, DVM
Crystal Ball: Predicting Foaling 63
   by Kenneth L. Marcella, DVM
Selection for the Miniature Horse Breeder 68
   by Toni M. Leland
C-Section in the Miniature Horse 73
   by Kenneth L. Marcella, DVM

Section IV—The Legal Side

Are You Really in Business? The IRS Wants To Know 77
   by Margaret Anderson Murphy
Transportation Coverage...Do Your Minis Need It?... 82
   by Margaret Anderson-Murphy

Section V—The Money Side: Buying or Selling

Buying & Selling Your Miniatures 85
    by Margaret Anderson-Murphy
Syndication 90
    by Cheryl A. Lekstrom & Margaret Anderson-Murphy
Top Notch Photos Sell Horses 99
    by Toni M. Leland

Section VI—Training & Showing Miniature Horses

Basics of Driving 105
    by Ted Garman
Sport Horse in Miniature 112
    by Cheryl A. Lekstrom
Raising A Well-Manner Foal 116
    by Katie Schubert

Section VII—Tools of the Trade: Your Tack & Equipment

Buying Used Vehicles 123
    by Bonnie Kreitler

Appendix

Additional Reading/Important Contacts 129
About the Authors 130
Standard of Perfection, AMHA & AMHR 131
Glossary 132
Other Titles/Order Form 135

THE BEGINNING

Miniature Horses in History
by Cheryl A. Lekstrom

The history of the Miniature Horse today is based on folklore, speculation, and varied fact–a result of gathering the bits and pieces of information from all over the world and melding them together.

THE FOLKLORE AND THE MYTHS

Helen S. Marble has raised Miniature Horses for over ten years at her Thistle Meadow Farm in Massachusetts. She gives the following account:

"The folklore is that [Miniature Horses] were bred in the 16th and 17th centuries in Europe. The European nobility would have their stable managers cross the smallest horses with each other and give [these small horses] as gifts. Conversely, the largest horses were crossed with each other during the Crusades, when the requirements of war called for animals that could haul armor-clad men with heavy weapons. During the famines and great wars in Europe, many Miniatures disappeared and it has been suggested that they were eaten. To make matters worse, with his large cavalry in mind, King Henry VIII of England ordered all stallions standing less than 14 hands high to be destroyed. Those that survived were hidden by their caretakers. Eventually these horses resurfaced in the company of gypsies and traveling circus performers who needed them for work. There were two different types: the refined type with slender long legs, delicate heads, and long necks and the smaller draft horse type that were stockier and broader with shorter necks. The stockier horses were preserved and used in the coal mines of England. Later on, they were imported into West Virginia, Kentucky, and Ohio where their size and strength made them ideal for work in the low-ceilinged mines."

Miniature Horses continued to be used in the mines of the southern states as recently as 1950.[1]

Myths concerning the origin of Miniature Horses are abundant. "One story has it that the little horses were found stranded in some box canyon, where years of short rations had reduced them to today's size. This imaginary canyon is variously reputed to be in Argentina or

Australia or the southwestern United States. ...Perhaps the most persistent fiction is that today's Mini is a throwback to *eohippus*, the "dawn horse" of the Eocene epoch—only 10 to 20 inches tall. (fig.1) Like its relatives the ancient tapir and rhinoceros, *eohippus* had four toes on its front feet, three on the rear, and teeth adapted to a forest diet of soft leaves. *Eohippus* died out about 50 million years ago in both North America and Europe. Fossil records mark the transition of [teeth and hooves] over the 50 million years since *eohippus*. [2]

fig. 1

THE FACTS AND SPECULATION

Originally, small horse breeds were usually the product of a severe natural environment where harsh climatic conditions and sparse feed contributed to their small stature. However, with a knowledge of genetics, it is also possible to breed specifically for size. We know for fact that, at various periods in equine history, Miniature Horses have been bred for pets, novelty, economy, veterinary research, and to show. We speculate that they are a product of nearly 400 years of selective breeding of many extracts, including that of English and Dutch mine horses. Although the Miniature Horses of today bear little resemblance to Shetland Ponies, undeniably, many do have Shetland ancestry. They are always referred to as miniature "horses," not ponies, because of their proportions, character and size. They are smaller than pony breeds.

"In the past decade, several breeders have imported Miniature Horses from England, Holland, Belgium, and West Germany, while others have selectively bred Miniatures from the larger breeds of horses. Although many purchases and breedings of Miniature Horses have been regularly documented in America since the early 1800's, accurate accounts and pedigrees were not maintained by most breeders until the 1940's." [3]

Actual documentation of the Miniature Horse goes back to the Renaissance period [14th to 16th centuries], but Miniature Horses have also been found buried in tombs with the Egyptian Pharaohs.[4]

History books mention that during the 1850's in France, the Empress Eugenie (wife of Napolean III) had a Miniature Horse to pull a small carriage. The palace children also had one or two for playmates. During the 1700's in England, small horses performed in traveling circuses. At

Astley's Circus, a small horse about 3-feet tall became popular for its mind-reading tricks. In another well-known circus act, a pair of small horses dressed up in hats sat down to take tea with the clowns.[5]

The first mention of a small horse being imported into the United States was in 1888 when a single pony out of 140 Shetlands turned out to be a 31-inch horse called *Yum Yum*. There was not much public awareness of true Miniatures during the years preceding 1960, although a few dwarfs became known, such as 23-inch *Tom Thumb* and a 26-inch mare called *Cactus*, as well as a few carnival freak-type small horses.[6]

THE FALABELLA BLOODLINE

Perhaps the most well-documented pedigree of the Miniature Horse is the Falabella bloodline. In most equine references and *The Encyclopedia of the Horse*[7], publishers refer to Miniature Horses as *Falabellas* [using the terms interchangeably].

Photo courtesy Lynn Cleare Goldman, North American Representative, Establecimientos Falabella

In 1845, an Irish horse-trader named Patrick Newtall traveled south of Buenos Aires, Argentina where he discovered a herd of unusually small horses grazing among the meadowlands. The Pampas Indians could not be precise about these horses' origin, but the animals had lived among their herds of Croillo horses for years. Newtall acquired several of these tiny horses from the Indians and began a breeding program. His son-in-law, Juan Falabella added European Throughbred bloodlines to the program for refinement. [In 1893, Juan included in his herd some Shetland specimens from the English or horses already smaller by selection, the Belgian or Dutch ones.] By the turn of the century, Juan Falabella was, through successive crossings, able to breed horses of good conformation with heights under 33.5 inches. In 1927, Juan's grandson, Julio Cesar Falabella, had a herd of several hundred Miniature Horses. He gained considerable publicity in 1962 when he sold a pair to the Kennedy family in this country.[8] Miniature Horses that are of the true Argentine Falabella stock are now registered with the Asociacion Argentina de Formento Equino & Asociacion de Criadores de Caballos Falabella.[9] The Establecimientos Falabella and all of their records were passed on to Maria Luisa Falabella upon the death of her husband Julio in 1980.[10]

THE FALABELLA COMES TO AMERICA

Many years ago, Jill Swedlow of Sunnyside Farm in California, interviewed the late Dixie Blasingame of Shadow Oaks Farm (California and Arkansas). She related the following story of how some of the first Falabella Mini Horses came to the United States.

A gentleman named John Aleno owned a farm adjoining the Falabella's ranch in Argentina. They were very good friends and it was because of this that Julio finally agreed to sell a few of his horses to Aleno... John Aleno used his small herd as a promotional gimmick for the Regina Winery in Etiwanda, California, where they were referred to as "Lilliputian Horses." They appeared in many parades pulling a scaled-down stagecoach bearing the winery's crest. They were also on view to the public. When Aleno died, the bank took over the horses as part of his estate. They were subsequently sold to a Mr. Fuller who had 600 acres of land in Running Springs, California. Fuller had the idea of turning his land into a recreation area, incorporating the Miniatures into the park. Unfortunately, some barriers were encountered when permission was needed to build an access road through government land. Their dream of having a recreational park was impossible, so the Fullers sold their horses and, since no outside stock had been brought in, the Falabella strain was kept pure.

FOUNDATION BREEDERS OF THE AMERICAN MINIATURE HORSE

In the early 1900's, **Normon Fields** of Bedford, Virginia began to buy pit ponies from Europe for use in the Appalachian coalmines. Sometimes he noticed very small horses among the ones that arrived in America. Fields kept the smallest horses and used them to raise his own herd. By 1964, he had 50 Miniature Horses in his herd, but most of them never left the area near his Virginia home.[11] He imported, bred, and raised Miniature Horses for 53 years.

Perhaps the person who did the most to develop and promote American Miniature Horses was the late **Walter Smith McCoy** of Rodderfield, West Virginia. The following is taken from his book, *The Story of the World's Smallest Ponies*.

In 1956, as a hobby, he collected all the ponies could find under 33 inches *"mostly for something to play with"* and because, *"I discovered that the smaller the ponies were, the more they sold for—usually five or six times as much as the large ponies would bring. After driving thousands of miles...I found 10 or 12 ponies that small. From those few ponies, by continually breeding the smallest down to the smallest, I now have one-hundred ponies under 32 inches tall, twenty of which are under 30 inches. These are Shetland Ponies; however, I think they can be called a special breed, since I have offered several times to bet $1,000 against $100 that I have the largest herd in the world under 32 inches tall, and have had no one to even say they doubted my claim. ...They are not knotty-headed dwarfs and are as good as the usual run of ponies throughout the United States...The colors are red, black, dappled, and spotted."* One of the smallest Miniatures ever bred was a mare named *Sugar Dumpling* who belonged to Smith McCoy. The horse was only 20 inches and weighed just 30 pounds. In 1967, he sold his herd of Miniature Horses to breeders all over the United States.

For over 30 years, **Alton V. Freeman** was a major zoo-animal importer for the United States. ...The original stock of the Freeman Mini Horses came from America's largest herd, owned by Smith McCoy. Forced to retire due to illness, Mr. McCoy sold Freeman about 40 head of his prime breeding stock, a collection accumulated by over 14 years of diligent searching, breeding, and selecting. Freeman had sold many of these animals during the course of his regular business as an exotic animal supplier before he realized the difficulties in getting breeding stock and the great demand for these little fellows. They were shipped all over the world: 15 went to Japan in repeat groups; 14 went to German breeders and the Frankfort Zoo; 5 went to a Swiss Zoo; 2 went to Universal Studios, and others went to individuals in Hawaii, Venezuela, Utica, Canada, Mexico, and Australia, including international financier Bernie Cornfeld in France.[12] McCoy's famous *Red Man* stallion (sold for $3,000), was purchased by the St. Louis Zoo in Missouri, where he stayed for two years. Alton Freeman bought the horse back and sold him in 1972 to Creekside Acres in North Carolina.

Moody & Lucy Bond of Bond's Miniature Horses in Lavonia, Georgia bred Minis for 45 years. *"It started as a hobby to see how small we could breed horses and still maintain good conformation."* To achieve their goal, the Bonds used *"trial and error—lots of it,"* said Lucy. Evidence of their success is her estimate that more than a thousand of the Miniatures in this country are descended from Bond stock.[13] A number of horses in the Bond herd were dispersed in 1992.

In 1974, **Mark Verhaeghe** came to America from his native Belgium. With 39 of his Miniature Horses, he founded Van't Huttenest Miniature Horse Farm in the Great Smoky Mountains in North Carolina. Verhaeghe is credited with bringing the "Dutch-bred Miniatures" into America. "Some of his horses can be traced back to the herd of two English sisters (both titled Lady Hope) who began to breed Miniatures in the 1860's." **J.C. Williams** of Dell Terra in Inman, South Carolina came to own *Field's Little Boy* and was the breeder of *Orion Light Van't Huttenest* (1974, 31" pintoloosa) now owned by Brewer Family Miniatures in Texas.

WINNING THEIR PLACE IN HISTORY

Vern Brewer was the patriarch of the Brewer Family Miniature Horse Farm in Gainesville, Texas, having built one of the best internationally-known herds of Miniature Horses in the country. Horses were a part of Vern's life since the mid-30's. A well-known Shetland Pony trainer, circus animal trainer, ringmaster, and high wire walker, Brewer started his Miniature Horse herd in 1981. He started with 6 yearlings by *Rowdy*, who was owned by his long-time friend, the late Ino W. Norman of Winters, TX. In the 1940's, Vern had trained Shetland Ponies for Norman, who later gave him the *Rowdy* fillies and a colt to get him interested in Miniatures. Vern Brewer left the farm to his family when he passed away in 1993. They did not want to disperse the herd, but kept it intact between family members. Brewer's top breeding stallions are the famous *Orion Light Van't Huttenest* and *Bond Dynamo*.[14]

Bob & Sandy Erwin dispersed NFC Farms in 1993 after 12 years of the most successful breeding, showing, and marketing program in the American history of Miniature Horses. No one can deny the dynamic force that NFC's marketing of *Hemlock Brooks Egyptian King, AMHA 4550* (31¼") and *Rowdy, AMHA 3622* (33¾") has had on the Miniature Horse industry. These two horses are the standard that most of today's breeders compare their horses against. These are the names that they look for in pedigrees of horses they buy to build their own herds. *Egyptian King*, with his classic gray Arabian profile, refinement, and grace is one of the leading sires of show winners and breeding stock today. *Rowdy* was a classic stallion with excellent conformation similar to that of a Thoroughbred. Without exception, his get are easily recognized as his, with their remarkable conformation and style. Many more elegant NFC Miniature Horses were dispersed to farms all across the United States and internationally.

MINIATURES IN THE FUTURE

The evolution of Miniature Horses has provided us with tiny replicas of Arabians, Thoroughbreds, Morgans, Quarter Horses, and draft-type horses, all with widely-varied degrees of refinement and good conformation. The quality of Miniature Horses in the show ring seems to be increasing exponentially every year. Horses that, three years ago would have been considered ten years ahead of their time, are abundant today. You can find these elegant horses from coast to coast. It isn't as though any one farm has the market share of them. Professional large horse enthusiasts have joined the ranks of Mini owners and breeders, and are quick to scrutinize and appreciate temperaments, colors, markings, symmetry, alignment, substance, quality, and performance potential.

As of October 1994, there were 58,259 Miniature Horses registered worldwide with the American Miniature Horse Association of Alvarado, Texas. Of those, 34,895 are mares, 21,187 are stallions, and 2,177 are geldings. Of the 6,054 members that make up the AMHA, 5,600 are from the United States and own 53,729 Mini horses. During 1994, 7,625 ownership transfers were made and, of these, 213 were geldings. We find them in small backyard herds in the suburbs and country, where they are perhaps replacing their larger breed cousins for reasons of economy. And, surprisingly, we find them in the city, where selectmen often don't hesitate to grant variances to accommodate them within their city limits.

Most of us are breeding Miniature Horses to sell as pets into a novelty market. We hope that our best ones will end up in the show ring with capable handlers who appreciate the delicate balance between size, correct conformation, and motion. The Miniature Horses of today are more refined and elegant than they have ever been. They bring great joy to all those who are lucky enough to know them.

No caption needed!

Bibliography

[1] "Miniature Horses: When The Short End of the Stick Is Better!," Cheri Jensen, Rocky Mountain Feed & Livestock Journal, *July 1993, pp 33-34.*

[2] "Miniature Horses," R. L. Blakely, National Geographic, *March 1985, p. 388.*

[3] The History of the American Miniature Horse, *American Miniature Horse Association.*

[4] "Miniature Horses: When The Short End of the Stick Is Better!," Cheri Jensen, Rocky Mountain Feed & Livestock Journal, *July 1993, pp 33-34.*

[5] The Miniature Horse, *Gail LaBonte, Dillon Press, Inc., 1990, pp 28-29.*

[6] The Freeman Mini Horse, *American Shetland Pony Journal, November 1973.*

[7] The Encyclopedia of the Horse, *Dorling Kindersely Publishing, New York, NY, 1994.*

[8] American Shetland Pony Journal, *November 1973.*

[9] New England Miniature Horse Society Miniature Horse Directory, *1994.*

[10] *Information from the Establecimientos Falabella provided by Lynne Cleare Goldman,* NEMHS Miniature Horse Directory, *1994.*

[11] The Miniature Horse, *Gail LaBonte, Dillon Press, Inc., 1990.*

[12] American Shetland Pony Journal, *November 1973.*

[13] "Miniature Horses," R. L. Blakely, National Geographic, *March 1985, p. 388.*

[14] "Goodbye, Dear Friend," Tony W. Greaves, Miniature Horse World, *April/May 1993, pp. 7 & 10; and 1991 Brewer Farm promotional material.*

SECTION 1
The Basics of Horse Ownership

HORSE KEEPING FOR THE NEWCOMER
by Toni M. Leland

Years ago, owning a horse was a luxury and those who could afford one left its care to the professional horseman. But today, more and more people with an average income are discovering the pleasure of owning a horse and many of them plan to or are keeping it on their own property. With Miniature Horses, this is especially appealing due to their small size and good personalities. However, they are still horses and must be cared for as such. Zoning regulations in towns throughout the country are being challenged constantly, as the controversy over the classification of these tiny equines goes on. A knowledge of good basic horse-keeping is a must to keep our towns from legislating horses as a nuisance. Many of the problems that we read about with regard to abuse and neglect are simply a matter of ignorance. Most people just don't know what is involved in keeping such an animal.

photo: Lorraine Mavrogeorge

BEFORE YOUR NEW MINIATURE HORSE ARRIVES

While the decision to buy a Miniature Horse is exciting, the first-time horse owner must take the time to insure that the arrival of this addition to the family has been well thought-out. Being prepared for the day the trailer rolls in the driveway is an exercise that can make or break the joy of the day. To care for your new horse on a day-to-day basis is not just a matter of being there to feed and water him. Certain supplies are needed and there are precautions to be taken <u>before</u> your Mini arrives. Horses are very sensitive to changes in their surroundings, pasture mates, humans, and daily routine. Making the transition from his old home to yours will be stressful, to say the least, but with a little foresight, you can help him acclimatize more easily. Once you have the preliminaries organized, you can go on to the finer points of keeping Miniature Horses.

Basic Supplies to Have on Hand

- 1 or 2 strong lead ropes with snap ends. Please don't use pet leashes. For all their small size, Miniature Horses still have a great deal of strength and need equipment that is meant for horses.
- A halter that fits. Talk to the seller and find out if your Mini's halter comes with him. If not, be sure to find out what size the owner uses for him and purchase one.
- A sturdy feed bucket that either hangs on the stall wall or a wide, flat one that is made to set on the ground.
- A sturdy water bucket for the stall and a large water tub for his turnout area.
- A curry comb, body brush, and mane/tail brush.
- A hoof pick.
- A manure rake and muck-bucket or wheelbarrow.
- Hay and grain. Be sure to ask the seller what he has been feeding your Miniature. If possible, get a small amount of the grain from the seller so that the transition from one feed to another does not upset your Mini any more than he is already.
- A telephone list by the phone that includes the seller and your veterinarian. In the event of an emergency, those numbers should be readily accessible to <u>anyone</u> who might need to make the phone call for you.

Basic checklist for the barn and turn-out/pasture

- A clean, well-bedded stall that has been inspected for nails, sharp edges, and places to get a foot caught. Check to make sure the stall door latches securely.
- Secure fencing that will keep him confined during his first few hours. If you have wire fencing, it would probably be a good idea not to turn him out until he has settled in for a day or so. With wire fencing, tie strips of colored plastic to the strands every 4-5 feet so that the horse can see it. On wooden fencing, make sure there are no sharp objects such as pieces of barbed wire or nails sticking out on the fencing, especially around the gate or area closest to where he came in. Make sure that the rails are spaced so that your Mini cannot walk under or climb through to escape. Remove any old trash or machinery on which he can injure himself.

WHY GOOD MANAGEMENT?

Good horse management should be the prime concern of all Miniature Horse owners for three very important reasons:
- First, and most important, is the health, comfort, and well-being of the horse.
- Second, is the acceptance of this hobby by the horse owner's immediate neighbors.
- Third, is the horse owner's pleasure.

WHERE YOUR MINI LIVES

Good common sense governs many of the problems we face with owning a horse. If you house your Miniature Horse in a tumble-down shed with a leaky roof and broken boards, he will eventually get into trouble. Colds or pneumonia, or a nasty cut or broken leg could be the price you (and your Mini) will pay for unsuitable stabling. So, your first concern should be safe, adequate housing. Nothing fancy, but it should be sturdy, well-ventilated (but draft-free), well lighted and large enough to provide a comfortable size stall. A 10' x 10' box stall is ideal for a Miniature Horse.

Keeping the barn light and airy will keep your Minis happier and healthier.

The ceiling should be high enough to allow good circulation of air. Unlike full-sized horses that can take advantage of the circulating air in the upper half of a building, Miniature Horses are trapped in the lower level of the barn. Without proper ventilation at this level, the air becomes stagnant, combining with stall fumes and ground dust to provide an unhealthy atmosphere. Respiratory and allergic problems can easily occur as a result. However, be sure that the ventilation is not so great as to be drafty. A horse standing in a cold, drafty stall for hours on end is prone to colds and respiratory problems.

The flooring should be level and provide drainage; there should be no water standing or running through the stall. Clay or dirt flooring is still considered one of the best footings for horses. Wood flooring tends to become slippery and smelly. If you use a board floor, be sure there is a slight separation between the boards to allow the urine to drain off.

Concrete is not a good option, but can be used in a stall if good deep bedding is used. Horses standing on concrete become stiff and sore, and such a floor certainly does not invite lying down! Clean stalls daily to prevent the buildup of manure and disease-producing bacteria, and always remove the old bedding from the building. Leaving wheelbarrows full of soiled bedding standing around adds to the smell and the fly population.

No horse will remain healthy and happy standing in a dank, dark stall for hours on end. The brighter and more cheerful the barn, the better. Take a stroll into the individual stalls every 3-4 days to assess them (especially with horses that are kept in all the time). Horses are wizards at unearthing things such as nails, wire, and similar objects on which to injure themselves.

Exercise is very important when keeping a horse. The turn-out area should be large enough to allow plenty of "horse play." Don't expect this area to also provide some of your horse's feed. A weed patch is not a pasture. Accept it for what it is—an area for exercise. Leaving your horses out all day is not a valid means of cutting down on the labor involved with keeping a clean barn. And it is not in the animals' best interest. You wouldn't like to spend hours in the hot sun chasing flies, or in a cold, pouring rain. When your Minis appear restless, bring them in for awhile or, if you don't have trees in the pasture, provide a "run-in shed" where they can doze in the shade. Night turnouts are usually better in the hot summer months. It is cooler and flies are less of a problem. Also, the horses' coats or tender muzzles won't get sunburned. Yes, sunburned. With Miniatures, depending on your area, the possibility of theft or wild animal danger might preclude leaving them out at night. Good fencing is a must if horses are to be turned out, and a certain amount of supervision is necessary.

FEEDING YOUR MINIATURE HORSE

Assuming that you purchased a healthy, sound animal, the best way to keep him that way is by correct feeding. Most horses will thrive on any one of the many well-balanced, pre-mixed feeds on the market today. Hay should be clean and sweet-smelling and be harvested at the time of its most nutritious growth. Hay can provide about 90% of the nutrients required by the horse if it is harvested young. Mature or idle horses can be maintained mostly on good hay alone. Never feed old, dusty hay—it will make your horses sick. Watch each bale carefully for mold. If you smell mold, shake the flake—fine dust will come out. NEVER give a horse moldy hay. You'll pay! If you find the remains of a mouse, rat, snake, or other creature inside a bale of hay, discard the <u>entire</u> <u>bale</u>—the consequences are not worth the risk. And don't try to use poor hay for bedding either, because horses being what they are, they are bound to nibble on it. While some horse owners like to use pelleted feed (a mix of grain and hay compressed into one form), it is a good idea to still provide hay or pasture to provide the roughage so essential to the horse's digestion. Having "something to do" also helps prevent stall vices such as chewing, windsucking, or kicking.

When to feed your horse is a question of significant importance. The horse's stomach can only handle relatively small amounts of food at one time. Mother Nature intended these grazing animals to nibble for most of their waking hours, so throwing feed in once a day, even if it is more convenient for you, is not a good idea. Your Miniature should be fed at least twice a day, preferably morning and evening, and at fairly regular times. A variation of a half-hour or so in the feeding time will not cause problems, but lack of a regular schedule will take it's toll on your horse's condition. "Poor keepers" (horses that require more than a normal diet to remain fit) or horses in poor condition will benefit from three daily feedings. Always consult your veterinarian if your horse is "off his feed," getting thin, or seems listless and droopy. A horse's appetite is an excellent gauge of his well-being.

Even more important than food is clean, fresh water. A horse deprived of water or on limited amounts will not be able to utilize his hay and grain to the best advantage. Free access to water is a must. Check your buckets daily and be sure they are cleaned regularly. During summer months, algae grows rapidly in water buckets and pasture tubs, fed by the small bits of grain, hay and saliva that get into the water and decompose. Most horses are extremely fussy about their water and will not drink stagnant water. In winter, keep the buckets unfrozen and add some warm water to the bucket; this ensures that your horse will drink what he needs. Often, ice-cold water can give a horse stomach distress.

A salt block should be placed in every horse's stall or be available to them on a free choice basis in the pasture or exercise area. Lack of salt in a horse's diet is evidenced by loss of appetite and, in some cases, severe debilitation.

Vitamin supplements are usually not required by a well-nourished mature horse. If you do think your horse can benefit from them, seek the advice of your veterinarian before administering supplements.

How much to feed? There is considerable lack of understanding in this area and many horses are either underfed or overfed. Any horse over three years of age must be fed on the basis of what he is doing, his age, and condition. Miniature Horses are considered "easy keepers," meaning that they do well on a normal diet. However, just like ponies, Miniatures can easily become overweight. The condition of the horse is the prime concern when determining how much to feed a horse. A horse hard at work requires more feed than the idle horse. "Hard at work" refers to being in training, or being used for pulling carts or carriages. A horse engaged in any athletic activity requires more energy and therefore more feed than a horse at pasture. Your Mini is in good condition if his rib cage cannot easily be seen, but can be felt when your hand is drawn along his side.

Watch your horses carefully, keeping track of weight and energy output; with this information you can plan a customized feeding program for each individual horse. One important point to remember is that the working horse left idle for more than one day should have his rations reduced by at least 1/3, or even half the normal amount if he remains idle for an extended period of time.

A good feeding procedure is to offer your horse his fresh water, then give him his hay and allow him 10 or 15 minutes of eating hay before graining him. Introduce any changes in feed gradually. Never allow a hot or upset horse to drink water or dive into his grain bucket. Walk the horse to cool him or settle him, then give him some hay to calm him down before allowing him the water and grain. To find out if your horse has cooled enough to drink, place your hand flat against his chest at the level of his legs. If the area feels hot to you, he is not cooled out enough and should not drink or eat.

THE NECESSARY EVILS

All horses have worms. A horse owner must try to keep the upper hand with a good worming program. Worms in horses is a prime cause of unthriftiness, poor digestion, anemia, loss of condition, and in severe cases, colic and possible death.

There are many worming drugs available and your veterinarian can best advise you on the most suitable program for your horse, in your specific area. The most important thing is that the drug be given regularly; worming twice a year is ineffectual. Three to four times per year is better and every two months is the most effective, because a new batch of worms matures every other month.

Signs of worm infestation include excessive thirst, manure-eating, dehydration, a large belly accompanied by ribs showing, listlessness, a poor, dull coat, rubbing the tail against walls and fences, and bouts of colic.

Do not administer worming medication if your horse is suffering from diarrhea or severe constipation, shows symptoms of colic, respiratory ailments, certain infectious diseases, or is under the influence of tranquilizers, muscle relaxants or other medications. If you have pregnant mares, consult your veterinarian as to which wormers to use and the timing of those wormings. The same applies to nursing mares and foals—your vet can guide you on this. When you schedule worming, plan to be around that day to observe for signs of a reaction. Always read the wormer labels carefully and follow the directions exactly. Use the proper amount of wormer based on the weight of the horse. Underdosing is ineffectual and over-dosing is downright dangerous.

KEEPING YOUR MINIS IMMUNIZED

Many horse diseases are preventable by the use of vaccinations. The most commonly used vaccinations are against equine influenza, Tetanus, rhinopneumonitis, and encephalomyelitis. In rural areas in some parts ofthe country, rabies shots are recommended, and for the public stable, strangles innoculation is almost always a must. In the eastern United States, Potomac Horse Fever has become a threat and there is a vaccine available for that. Vaccination schedules usually revolve around spring and fall doses, but this again is dependent upon the area in which you keep your horses. Your veterinarian can set up the appropriate schedule for you.

ON-GOING HORSE CARE

Your Miniature Horse's feet should be picked out daily. Keep his bedding clean and dry to prevent the very common problem of thrush, an infection caused by lack of proper cleanliness of the hoof and prolonged contact with wet bedding. The signs of this disease are a foul-smelling, blackish discharge from the frog of the horse's foot. Regular hoof trimming is necessary, especially for horses that stay inside most of the time. If you live in a very dry area, you might ask your farrier about hoof dressing to preserve the moisture in the foot and keep the hoof soft and pliable so that cracks won't develop.

Check your horse's teeth regularly to determine if sharp edges are present and, if so, have your veterinarian "float" these edges off. How often this is required will be determined by the age of the horse and his diet. Sharp edges on teeth will cause the horse to have a sore mouth and he will chew or eat incorrectly. Signs of a horse with tooth problems include grain scattered on the floor under the bucket, undigested grain passed through in the manure, digestive disturbances, loss of condition, and in the case of a horse that is using a bit, head-tossing and lack of cooperation when being worked. (see *Understanding Teeth*," page 43)

A well-groomed Miniature Horse looks beautiful and is healthier. Thorough and regular grooming is necessary to help prevent sores caused by sweat and salt on the body after working, especially under harness. Mud left on the legs causes irritation and the condition called scratches. A clean, healthy horse also seems to utilize his food better. Bathing should never replace the curry comb and brush that works to improve the circulation and remove old, dried skin. An occasional bath can be very refreshing in the summer and, if you are showing your Minis, is necessary to get the best look possible. Bathing should never be attempted when the horse is overheated. Sponge down the legs with tepid water to help cool an overheated horse. Since your horse's coat is an indication of his general health, the care given to his feeding and grooming is very important. There are no shortcuts to a good coat on your horse. A small amount of corn oil (about 2 oz.) added to his daily feed will help in the shedding-out process in the spring, and help give gloss to a clean coat.

YOU AND THE NEIGHBORS

Good management of your Miniature Horse is in everyone's best interest. A healthy horse is more economical to own, is of more service and enjoyment to his owner, and when kept under controlled conditions in clean, sanitary surroundings, is less likely to disturb the immediate neighbors. Good horse-keeping can help dispel the prejudices and arguments against keeping them in urban areas. The Miniature Horse has played a great part in this area of change.

As a horse owner, you are obligated to do the very best you can toward caring for your animals in a responsible, humane way. Even though they are so much smaller than their big cousins, they are still equines and can be viewed as a nuisance and/or a health hazard in a non-agricultural area.

Keeping Your Mini in The Backyard—
Will Your Local Zoning Allow It?
by Attorney Margaret Anderson-Murphy

Before you buy your first Miniature Horse, you must decide where he will live. For many people, the answer appears to be obvious: the new member of the family will occupy the fenced area that was formerly the vegetable garden, or will inhabit a corner of the garage (although this is not necessarily a recommended practice). Before you dump a load of shavings onto the garage floor or reinforce your existing fencing, make a trip to your local Town Hall to check out your town's zoning regulations. While each state passes laws that enable towns and cities to pass zoning regulations, the actual content of those regulations varies from town to town.

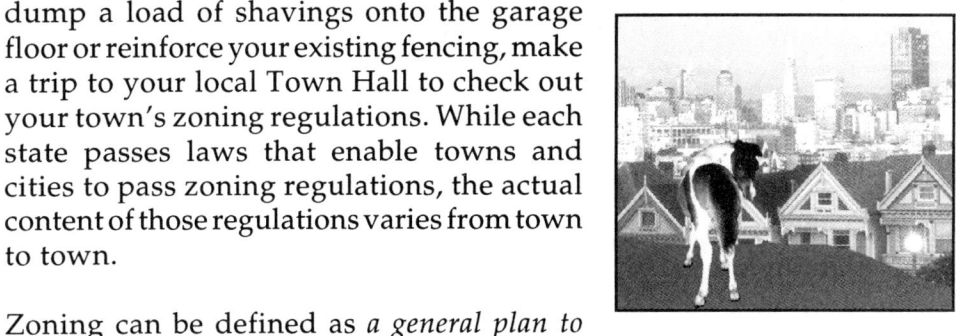

Zoning can be defined as *a general plan to control and direct the use and development of property in a town or city, or a large part thereof, by dividing the town into districts according to the present and potential use of the property.* Keeping this in mind, consider the neighborhood in which you live. If you live in a rural area and some or all of your neighbors keep full-sized horses or other types of livestock that are typically raised on a farm, the addition of a Miniature Horse to your backyard may not be in violation of your zoning ordinances. If, however, you live in a neighborhood that is somewhat suburban and the largest animal on your block is your neighbor's Great Dane, keeping a horse in the backyard, no matter how small he is, may present problems for you.

Once you have obtained a copy of your local zoning ordinances, review any provisions in those ordinances which refer to horses, livestock, pets and/or animals in general. Because Minis have become so popular only recently, it is very likely that your local zoning commission has not formulated a specific provision to deal with their stabling. However, towns with agricultural property may have specific requirements for keeping horses or livestock that call for a minimum acreage or a minimum setback from property lines.

WHAT THE COURTS SAY

Examine the uses which are permitted in the district in which your property lies. If your property does not meet the requirements for keeping a full-sized horse, you can make the argument that keeping a Miniature Horse on your property is an *accessory use* of your residential property. An accessory use is one which is customarily incidental and subordinate to and dependent on the principal use of a building or property. When courts have had to review this issue, they have looked at factors such as the size of the lot in question, the nature of the primary building on the property or the use made of adjoining lots; the economic structure of the entire area; and, the incidence of similar uses in the vicinity of the particular property in question. Courts may also consider the actual or potential detriment to the neighborhood's residential character as well.

Because of their size and because of the fact that Minis do not require as large a turnout area as would a full-sized horse, it is possible to make the argument that the horse is being kept strictly as a pet and is therefore a permitted accessory use under the zoning regulations. At least one court has held that keeping a full-sized pig as a pet was an accessory use because the court looked at the nature of the use of the animal, rather than its usual classification as livestock. In that case, the pig was kept like a pet and was not kept for sale, stud purposes, or food. It was clean and inoffensive and it was petted by the owners, their children, and their neighbors. The court based its reasoning in part upon the fact that the ordinance of the town in question did not prohibit unusual pets. With regard to horses, there have been cases where courts have reviewed whether stabling a horse on residentially-zoned property was a practice customarily associated with residential living in the area and was therefore a permitted use within the zoning regulations.

Keep in mind that we are talking about keeping one or two Miniature Horses strictly for personal use and that we are not talking about keeping these horses for commercial use, such as the boarding of other people's horses or breeding purposes. If you intend to use your property for a potentially-profitable use of Miniatures, you should check the commercial zoning requirements as well. If it is a use specifically prohibited by the zoning in question, it will be necessary for you to go before the zoning board and seek what is known as a *variance* in order to conduct the prohibited activity on your property.

TALKING TO THE ZONING BOARD

If you find the need to make an application to your local zoning board to keep one or more Miniature Horses, prepare in advance by having satisfactory solutions to any of the potential problems raised by any of the zoning board members. Regardless of whether you are planning to keep your Mini in your garage or planning to build him his own barn, you should ask your surrounding neighbors how they would feel about sharing the neighborhood with a Miniature Horse. If you need to go before the zoning board to obtain permission to keep a Mini at your house, obviously you will be better off if you could represent to the board that your neighbors have no objection to you keeping a Miniature Horse on your property and, if any of them do object, you can address their concerns prior to the hearing and smooth the road for your application to be approved. You may wish to retain a lawyer who is familiar with zoning procedures to assist you. Because most people are not familiar with Miniature Horses, the word "horse" will immediately conjure up visions of flies, manure, and trampled lawns in proportion to a full-sized horse. This is not to imply that a Miniature Horse does not or cannot generate any of the above nuisances, but since the proportions are obviously smaller, with careful maintenance, these problems need not be a problem to the neighbors. If you know of other Miniature Horse owners in the neighboring towns who are keeping their Minis in a residential setting, try to obtain information about their situations and discuss this information with the zoning board, if possible. Pictures of the horses and the property in question may also be helpful if the zoning board is willing to review them.

Because the regulations vary from town to town, and because each case is fact-specific, it is possible that two neighboring towns can come down with completely different rulings on keeping a Miniature Horse in the backyard. If you need to go before your zoning board, be prepared with your arguments and be ready to educate the zoning board members regarding Minis.

Finally, regardless of what is permitted by zoning, be sure that the set-up that you are considering for your Miniature Horse is humane and in his best interests. After all, his safety and welfare are the most important facts to remember.

Reprinted from Eastern Miniature, January 1992

Perilous Pasture Plants
by Cindy Fisher

Over 700 North American plant species are known to be toxic to man and beast, although reactions vary from one species to another. Most toxic plants offer the curious nibbler a bitter taste or a prickly sensation, but some are quite palatable. Sometimes a horse will graze with impunity close to toxic plants, or even develop a taste for them.

A horse's age, the time of year, your soil type, and climatic conditions all greatly alter the production of toxins in plants. Plant poisoning is most likely to occur when forage is scarce or the paddock is overcrowded. Curiously, plant poisoning in horses is more common Out West than in The East.

While some poisonous plants are fairly common, many are uncommon ones and therefore are not readily recognized by horse owners. Here is a list of plants your horses should avoid, and the symptoms and disorders they can cause:

SUDAN GRASS *(Sorghum sudanense)* in the green growth stage, especially if stunted by drought, is extremely toxic and can cause urinary incontinence, bladder inflammation, and muscular incoordination. Once this plant matures to 18 inches it is no longer considered a threat.

ALSIKE CLOVER *(Trifolium hybridum)* **(a)** may cause liver damage. In bright, sunny weather, a photosensitive reaction causes the affected horse's muzzle and feet to become red and irritated. Sores may appear inside the mouth, and nervous and digestive disorders may occur.

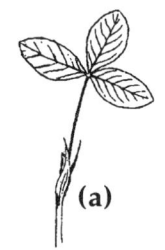

LEAFY SPURGE *(Euphorbia esula)* may irritate the digestive tract. Horses standing in paddocks heavy in leafy spurge may suffer from burns to the skin around their feet.

BRACKEN FERN *(Pteridium aquilinum)* **(b)**, perhaps ingested from contaminated hay or bedding, causes weight loss, staggering, muscle tremors, and loss of appetite. An enzyme in this fern slowly destroys the body's thiamine (vitamin B-1), causing signs that may not be apparent for up to three months. Vitamin B-1 injections, given in time, can reverse the problem.

HORSETAIL *(Equisetum arvense)* **(c)** is similar to bracken fern in destroying vitamin B-1 and the resulting symptoms it causes.

ST. JOHN'S WORT *(Hypericum performatum)* **(d)**, in both shrub and herb form, contains a pigment that is absorbed through the intestinal wall, but is not eliminated through the liver or kidneys. This plant causes intense itching and hypersensitivity to light. In severe cases, the horse may charge about as if mad. Dark skinned horses are less affected than lighter horses.

GROUND IVY *(Glechoma hederacea)* **(e)** causes slobbering, sweating, and pupil dilation. In severe cases, fluid accumulates in the lungs, causing death.

BLACK CHERRY *(Prunus serotina)* leaves **(f)**—both wild and cultivated trees—contain deadly cyanide, which attacks the respiratory system and causes gasping, convulsions, and suffocation.

MOUNTAIN LAUREL *(Kalmia latifolia)* **(g)**, a multi-branched shrub or small tree 3- to 15-feet high, causes labored breathing, nausea, constipation, diarrhea, and death in horses.

NIGHTSHADE *(Solanum dulcamera)***(h)** and **RHODODENDRON** *(Rhododendron maximum)* both produce the same symptoms as Mountain Laurel. The genus Solanum contains a number of cultivated species, native weeds, and introduced plants that, if ingested, cause weakness, trembling, nausea, constipation, diarrhea, and possibly death. Other species in this family include:
- BLACK, DEADLY, or GARDEN NIGHTSHADE *(S. nigrum Linnaeus)*, a common weed with white flowers and black berries

- SAND BRIER *(S. carolinense Linnaeus)*, with its prickly stems and leaves, and smooth orange-yellow berries
- SAND BUR *(S. rostratum Dunal)* with 1" wide yellow flowers, prickly stems and leaves, and each berry enclosed in a prickly calyx
- POTATO *(S. tuberosum Linnaeus)*, the best known member of the Solanum family
- TOMATO (Lycoperiscon lycopersicum), although not in the same genus, is related and is similarly toxic.

HORSERADISH *(Armoracia rusticana)*, a hot and spicy delight cultivated commercially and in home gardens, can be found growing wild and perennially in temperate climates. In a horse's stomach, this condiment can cause acute inflammation of the mucous membrane. The horse may become excited, experience pain, and lose weight, even though he continues to eat well. The final result is often collapse and death.

FOXGLOVE *(Digitalis purpurea)* **(j)** can be fatal if ingested in large amounts. The dried leaves of this popular garden flower are used to make digitalis, the powerful heart stimulant and diuretic.   (j)

JIMSONWEED, or **THORNAPPLE** *(Datura stramonium)* **(k)**, can be fatal if eaten in large amounts, as the roots contain atropine, a drug used for medicinal purposes.

JAPANESE YEW *(Taxus cuspidata)*, an ornamental bush, causes almost instant death in horses, although deer can eat it with no ill effects.

OAK *(Quercus rubra)* contains tannic acid and volatile oil in its leaves and acorns that can cause poisoning as long as seven days after being eaten by a horse.

An ounce of prevention, as they say, is worth a pound of cure. To prevent poisoning, regularly check paddocks, fields, and meadows for toxic plants. Provide your horses with sufficient hay and grain to keep hunger from tempting them to nibble on questionable plants. Grazing your horse or pony on the lawn may be amusing, but the vegetable and flower beds surrounding lawns all too often harbor potential toxins.

DANGER FROM OTHER QUARTERS

Kind but unsuspecting cooks or gardeners who indiscriminately feed their animals vegetable cuttings could be putting their equines in grave danger. Seeds and cuttings from kitchen and garden belong in a compost heap, well away from curious equine lips.

Perhaps the greatest danger to a horse or pony comes in the form of family, friends, and curious passersby who, thrilled at the thought of feeding a farm animal over the paddock fence, may grab handfuls of flowers and weeds at the roadside for the delighted equines eagerly waiting to receive them.

So, despite your most diligent measures, accidents happen. To make matters worse, a horse may become sick weeks or months after ingesting a toxic plant. By the time the central nervous system is affected, the animal is likely beyond treatment. Speed is therefore of the utmost importance when treating toxicosis.

OTHER TOXINS

Toxic plants and weeds aren't the only potentially dangerous materials found near horses. Equine health and medical products can be, and often are, overused by owners and groomers. Take care to avoid the over-application or overdose of vitamins, dewormers, and other health-care products.

Insecticides, rodenticides, and other pesticides are manufactured and distributed under a vast array of names and sold for a myriad of purposes. If you use such products, carefully read the labels and follow all directions. Store the products away from horses, under lock and key, or well out of reach of any horse or pony that successfully opens stall or stable doors.

WHAT TO DO

Suspect plant poisoning if your horse exhibits signs of gastrointestinal disorder (pawing or kicking at his abdomen, getting up and down, rolling, watching his flank, dog-sitting and other abnormal postures), nervousness, sudden collapse, or death. Short of the latter, move the horse from the paddock or field where the suspected poison grows. Keep him warm and retain samples of blood, urine, and feces for analysis by your veterinarian.

If the horse is unconscious or anesthetized, a gastric lavage (wash) may be necessary. Otherwise, a laxative consisting of 6 pints of mineral oil administered by mouth, should be sufficient to empty his digestive tract. Follow this treatment with a *slurry* (a watery mixture of insoluble matter) made up of 500 gm of activated charcoal in a gallon of warm water.

In cases of skin exposure, wash the affected skin with a mild detergent and plenty of clear water.

If you can determine which plant poisoned your horse, your vet may be able to recommend a specific antidote. Otherwise, treatment must be based on visible symptoms. Either way, watch your horse carefully until he recovers.

Reprinted by permission of Rural Heritage magazine, Spring 1995.

More Toxic Plants and Their Effects

CASTOR BEAN *(Ricinus communis)*: intestinal irritation

CHIVES *(Allium soboenoprasm)*: liver and kidney degeneration

FIDDLENECK *(Ansinckia intermedia)*: liver cirrhosis

GOLDEN WEED *(Onopis spp)*: selenium poisoning

LOCOWEED *(Astragalus spp)*: nervous system damage

OLEANDER *(Nerium oleander)*: digitalis effect

PRINCE'S PLUME *(Stanleya spp)*: selenium poisoning

RATTLEWEED *(Crotalari spectabilis)*: liver cirrhosis

RUSSIAN KNAPWEED *(Centaurea repens)*: encephalomalacia

TANSY RAGWORT *(Senecio jacondaea)*: liver cirrhosis

WHITEHEAD *(Sphenosciodium capitallatum)*: photosensitivity

WILD ONION *(Allium validum)*: hemolytic anemia

WILD TOBACCO *(Nicotiana trigonophylla)*: paralysis

WOODY ASTER *(Zylorrheza spp)*: selenium poisoning

YELLOW STAR THISTLE *(Centaurea solstitialis)*: encephalomalacia

---

For additional information on poison plants and substances toxic to horses, see *"Poisonous Plants: A Survival Guide,"* <u>Equus</u>, June 1995, pp.28-37.

Using The Right Words:
Pedigree & Breeding Terminology
by Susan Larkin

The proper use of terminology when dealing with any aspect of the horse business is important. For instance, when a breeder places an ad and uses improper terms when describing his or her stallion, it leads the informed mare owner to believe this person is at least partially ignorant of breeding terminology, and possibly neglectful in other areas of the horse business. An advertisement for horses for sale is also a common place to find the improper use of horse terms. It is normal for knowledgeable persons to assume these people are uninformed, in the least. In these competitive times, everyone wants an edge. A horseperson who at least appears to be well-versed in proper terminology will have the advantage over the person who uses improper terms. Mare owners can be real picky when it comes to the care and management of their horses. And with good reason. There is considerable time and expense involved with sending your mare out to be bred, and you expect her (and possibly her foal at side) to be well-cared for by informed professionals. Your impression of these professionals includes the use of proper terminology.

On the other hand, misuse of horse terminology doesn't always indicate lack of knowledge in many other areas of horse breeding. It just might appear that way to some. It would show me that this person doesn't pay particular attention to detail or doesn't wish to become more knowledgeable, or hasn't had the opportunity yet to learn, all of which might affect the way my mare is cared for. I'm probably going to step on a lot of toes here, but I feel strongly enough about the proper use of these terms to at least try and explain them.

I have found that the improper use of "**by**" and "**out of**" a particular horse is misused more often by the majority of people than any other term. I hear the phrase *"my horse is out of (a famous stallion)"* from people who really should know better. These are fairly knowledgeable horsemen from an outward appearance. This "famous stallion" is usually not even the sire, and is often several generations back in the horse's pedigree. Correctly used, "by" refers to the sire of the horse, and "out of" refers to the dam. It's easy to remember "out of" as literally "out of a mare." These terms should not be used any other way.

Another case of misuse is using a famous horse's name to describe your horse, as in *"my Bond Anthony mare."* This term, if correctly used, would imply that the mare is a direct daughter of *Bond Anthony*. Usually, the pedigree of the mare would reveal that *Bond Anthony* is at least a grandparent, if not farther back. If this is the case, the proper term would be *"my Bond Anthony-bred mare,"* if you didn't want to use a name closer up in the pedigree. Are we so afraid of mentioning the immediate horses in the pedigree that we don't say who they are, and grab for a famous name farther back in the bloodline? I find that this is the case with a lot of people. They are afraid you will think their horse is lesser-bred if they say a name you don't know. Except in the cases of very well-bred, expensive horses, most horses are a couple of generations away from a well-known horse. If the sire of your horse is unknown to most people, you could say your horse is *"by a son of Bond Anthony,"* or *"out of a granddaughter of Bond Anthony,"* if you want to use *"Bond Anthony"* in reciting your horse's bloodline. This would be correct terminology.

RELATIVES

Using the words "**full brother or sister**" and "**half-brother or sister**" are also misused when describing the bloodlines of our horses. The term "full brother or sister to *FMA War Paint*," for example, means that this horse has both of the same parents as *FMA War Paint*. "Half-brother or sister" means that this horse is out of the same mare as *FMA War Paint*, but by a different sire. I know, both parents are 50% of the blood of the foal; at least we think so genetically. And yes, technically, a foal of *FMA War Paint* is a half-brother to all the other foals by *FMA War Paint*. But this usage of terminology is incorrect when describing your horse's parentage. A stallion sires many, many foals a year and, in many cases, these foals are usually out of lesser-bred mares than the stallion. There will be a small percentage of really good horses coming from any given foal crop of a stallion; these foals will have only a small resemblance to each other. However, a mare produces one foal a year and her foals will have many common characteristics, even if they're by different sires. Just because your horse is by a particularly famous stallion, and this famous stallion has sired a number of exceptional horses, doesn't automatically mean your horse is just as good as those other exceptional horses. One would like to think they are as good, and sometimes they're right. But referring to your horse as a "half-brother to" one of these exceptional horses by the same sire is incorrect.

More importantly, the term "half-brother or sister" refers to horses from the same mare, and holds more weight in performance and breeding terms. The stud books, sale catalogs, breeding articles and reference books all have used this terminology for several hundred years. Correctly used, when describing your horse as a *"half-brother or sister to so-and-so,"* you are describing a horse who has more importance performance-wise or breeding-wise than the half-brother by the same sire only. Many people disagree with this, and speaking in blood, the horses by the same sire being called half-brothers and half-sisters is correct, and the degree of relationship is the same (50%) as it is if they were from the same mare and by a different sire. I'm only stating this in the terms generally accepted throughout the world.

Another example: suppose you have a horse by *Happy Appy*, and out of a daughter of *NFC Egyptian King's Keepsake*. And there is another horse out there who is well-known and he is also by *Happy Appy*, but from a different daughter of *Egyptian King's Keepsake*. You could say your horse is a *"three-quarter brother in blood to this horse."* Many use this descriptive term to show, in percentage of blood, how much a certain horse is bred like another. A colt by *Orion-Light Van't Huttenest*, out of a full sister to *Umbrella-Bird Van't Huttenest* (*Happy Appy's* dam) would be considered a full brother in blood to *Happy Appy* (who is *by Orion-Light Van't Huttenest*). (fig. 1) This is correct terminology. If you have a horse by *Happy Appy*, you do not have a half-brother or half-sister to all the other foals by *Happy Appy*. In blood you do, but in correct terminology, you do not.

Now, if you had a "half-brother to *Happy Appy*," this would mean your horse is out of the same mare as *Happy Appy*, and in my opinion, would be more important in terms of a performance/breeding animal than if this horse was only by *Orion Light Van't Huttenest* (the sire of *Happy Appy*). Now, *"only by Orion Light Van't Huttenest"* shouldn't be taken to mean a lesser horse. The horse just might be a better horse. But only genetics and transmitted genes to the foal determine this. We have no way of knowing the outcome of a mating before the foal is born. And the sheer numbers, in terms of a stallion's foals as opposed to a mare's foals, require that correct terminology be

---

HAPPY APPY **
    Orion Light Van't Huttenest
    Umbrella-Bird Van't Huttenest

COLT**
    Orion Light Van't Huttenest
    Full Sister to Umbrella-Bird Van't Huttenest

** These two horses are full brothers in blood

fig. 1: Pedigree-form showing relation between full brothers used to describe an animal's parentage. "**Half-siblings**" immediately tells you they are out of the same mare. Using "half-siblings" to mean by the same sire would require more information to differentiate this horse from all other foals by this same sire, which could number up to hundreds.

OFFSPRING

Using the word "**producer**" to describe a stallion's breeding accomplishments is also incorrect. A "producer" is the correct term to describe a mare's produce. "**Progeny**" refers to a stallion's foals, and is also sometimes used to describe a mare's foals, although not often. The word "**get**" is also used in reference to a stallion's foals. Instead of using "this stallion is a good producer," you might use "this stallion is a good sire," or *"a progenitor."* "Producer" should only be used as in "this mare is a good producer," or "this mare line is a producing one." The term "produce" and "offspring" can also refer to all foals by a sire or a mare, generally speaking, but I think that the word "foals" would better describe all the get of a sire, as in "his foals are good runners."

"Granddaughter of FWF Little Blue" and *"grandson of FWF Little Blue,"* when generally used, leaves open a couple of possibilities. Is this horse by a son of *Little Blue*, or out of a daughter of *Little Blue*? If he is by a son of *Little Blue*, then you could say "a grandson of *Little Blue*," or a "paternal grandson of *Little Blue*." If he is out of a mare by *Little Blue*, the term would be "a maternal grandson of *Little Blue*," or "out of a daughter of *Little Blue*." And, yes, technically he would be a grandson either way. The term "great-grandson of" refers to the horses in the third generation of the pedigree, with the words "**paternal**" referring to the sire's side, and "**maternal**" referring to the dam's side of the pedigree.

PEDIGREES

In looking at a pedigree form, however laid out, the sire should always be shown as the top half of the pair that results in a foal, and should remain so throughout the pedigree, no matter how many generations back you go. All breed associations do this on horses' registration papers that show a pedigree for at least 2 generations, as does anyone who traces pedigrees professionally. An example two generations is shown in figure 2.

The generally accepted terminology in describing pedigrees when referring to the number of generations, is to not count the subject horse

	1st Generation	**2nd Generation**
		stallion (grandsire or paternal grandsire)
	stallion (sire)	Mare (paternal granddam)
Your Horse		
	mare (dam)	stallion (maternal grandsire)
fig. 2		mare (maternal granddam or 2nd dam)

as a "generation" (though technically it is). When you hear or see the term, "five-generation pedigree," or "five-cross pedigree," it usually refers to the subject horse, plus five generations of ancestors, for a total of 63 horses. Each generation back doubles in the number of horses it contains, with the 2nd generation containing 4 horses, the 3rd generation containing 8 horses, the 4th containing 16, and so on. Sometimes a short pedigree is written out like this: **horse (sire x dam, dam's sire)**
This is often sufficient when describing to another person a horse's breeding. The sire and the dam's sire are usually considered enough evidence of a horse's pedigree when someone is inquiring about his bloodlines. These two stallions are usually well-known, so their names are used instead of the mares' names in the pedigree.

The degree of "**inbreeding**" would affect the number of "common ancestors" in a pedigree. The term, "inbreeding" refers to taking a stallion of certain blood and crossing it with a mare of the same blood. The degree of "inbreeding" can be close, or far removed many generations (which is sometimes referred to as "**linebreeding**"). You can study a good example of linebreeding/inbreeding when looking at the pedigrees of horses bred by Hank Weiscamp (breeder of the famous Quarter Horse, *Skipper W*). "**Common ancestors**" is the term used to describe horses repeated within a pedigree, however close or far back they are. It is rare to find a purebloodeed horse (Arabian, Thoroughbred, etc.) who does not have any common ancestors within the first 5 generations of his pedigree. History shows that inbreeding within the first 2 generations has been done with Arabians more than other breeds. [Ed.note: Due to the relatively recent popularity of Miniature Horses, inbreeding was practiced heavily in the beginning, resulting in a limited gene pool. Therefore, it is not unusual to find common ancestors in the first two generations of a Miniature Horse pedigree.] In Miniature Horses, the specialization of certain types and selecting for small size dictate the use of a limited gene pool. Hopefully, this use of concentrated genes (inbreeding) is used with caution, using only superior individuals, since you risk receiving the undesirable traits along with the desirable ones. When only the desirable traits remain dominant in the resulting foal, you will have a superior individual.

"**Outcrossing**" is the practice of breeding two individuals who have no common ancestors for 5 or 6 generations or more. This practice is often successful at regular intervals within a pedigree when combined with close inbreeding. Sometimes outcrossing produces what is called "**hybrid vigor**." Hybrid vigor is described as superior performance gained from an influx of new blood to the genetic makeup of a certain individual. This "new blood" also has to be of superior stock in itself, just as with inbreeding to a particular superior individual, to produce a horse with desirable traits.

"**Tail male line**" and "**tail female line**" are terms used to describe the top and bottom lines of a horse's pedigree. "Tail male line" is the descending or ascending line of sires from a particular horse. "Tail female line" refers to the dam's line back to a certain individual mare, as in the dam's dam's dam, etc. The terms "1st dam," "2nd dam," "3rd dam," are used to identify the mare's position in the pedigree. The 1st dam would be the horse's dam, the 2nd dam would be the maternal granddam (the 2nd generation), the 3rd dam would be the third mare down the tail female line, and so on.

"**Nicking**" refers to known successful crosses of two particular bloodlines. "Nicks" are used by many breeders who don't wish to risk their resources on crosses they can't predict or when they simply like the cross of these lines. If it's been successful in the past, chances are it will be successful again. The cross of Thoroughbred stallion *Three Bars* on daughters of *Leo* was well-documented as being successful. So was the cross of Thoroughbred *Bold Ruler* on daughters of **Princequillo*. But, daughters of *Buckpasser* didn't cross well with *Bold Ruler* (unsoundness problems). Quarter Horse *Freckles Playboy* crosses well with daughters of *Doc O'Lena* and so did *Pretty Boy* on daughters of *Blackburn*. These are some of the many successful nicks in other breeds. Discovering the ones that are not yet well-known for Miniature Horses can be very rewarding for breeders.

"**Broodmare sire**" is a term used to describe the sire of the dam of a horse. When it is said that a horse is a good "broodmare sire," it means that his daughters are successful producers. Most stallions that are considered to be successful can attribute that success to at least one of three things: he's a good sire of performers, a good sire of sires, or a good broodmare sire. And, in most cases, this stallion was at least a moderate performer himself.

NFC's Rowdy is an excellent example of a Miniature Horse stallion who was all three — sire of good performers, sire of good sires, and a good broodmare sire. Racing Thoroughbred *Secretariat* turned out to be one of the leading broodmare sires, yet his sons are considered failures at stud. *Man O'War, Princequillo, War Admiral, Depth Charge*, and countless other famous stallions were also considered to be excellent broodmare sires, but not the best sires of sires.

Most people would agree that more emphasis is placed on the stallion to be the exceptional one of the pair to be bred. He is usually the one with the great performance record or a great siring record, and is usually better-bred than the mares to which he is mated. He sires more foals per year and the attention is on him through sheer numbers of his foals. If at least the same importance was placed upon the mares we use to produce our foals, our yearly foal crops would contain more than the current 5% superior individuals. Most of these superior stallions have superior dams. If his dam did not perform, then she was usually superbly-bred, or superbly-conformed. If a stallion to be used for breeding should have the well-known 4 ingredients to be a successful stallion (performance, breeding, conformation, and temperament), then why not require as much from a broodmare? They are at least 50% of the foal, and I think they contribute more than 50%, in terms of influence on the foal.

There are very few really superior stallions out there who are out of poor mares. Sale catalog pages are filled with information pertaining to the performance and produce of the immediate female lines. There is mention of the sire's performance and get, and maybe his sire, but nothing is said of the horses in the middle of the pedigree. Brilliant performing mares will usually be successful as broodmares, often producing males capable of being successful sires. In the Quarter Horse and Thoroughbred racing world, the champion running mares usually produce superior performance horses, and even produce world-class sires.

Please educate yourself in the proper usage of pedigree and breeding terminology. It may seem trivial, but it will only serve to enhance your reputation as a breeder of fine horses, and your success as a horseperson in general.

Reprinted with permission from the author & Southwestern Horseman, March 1995.

It's 10 pm . . .
Do You Know Where Your Minis Are?
by Bonnie Kreitler

Although no federal agency or insurance industry association compiles statistics on stolen horses, horsemen across the country have the uneasy sense that horse thievery is on the rise. In some states like Texas which have large horse populations and which have been hard hit by the economic downturn, they describe the problem with words like epidemic and rampant. A few of these missing horses may be destined for a clandestine career in someone else's barn. But the greater likelihood is that they are on their way to a backwater auction or to a slaughterhouse.

Robin Lohnes, executive director of the American Horse Protection Association (AHPA) in Washington, D.C., speculates that modern day rustlers, pinched by job layoffs or other economic problems, see horses as a ready source of non-taxable cash income. There are fourteen slaughterhouses in the United States processing horse meat for human consumption overseas, she points out. Furthermore, there is no federal requirement that proof of ownership be produced before a sales transactions takes place. Not surprisingly, theft reports received by AHPA appear to be more numerous in regions within easy driving distance of these plants.

Slaughterhouses accepting horses that will end up in dog food cans may pay less than 10 cents per pound for the horses they buy. Hardly an incentive to break the law. But packing plants sending horse meat to European butcher shops pay far more. When horse meat prices reach the 70 to 80 cents per pound range, a 1000 pound horse is worth $700 to $800 at the packing plant. At those prices, more auction horses head to the killers and more thieves are tempted to go into action.

The U.S. Department of Agriculture reports that some 315,000 horses were slaughtered in 1990 for both human and non-human consumption.

These animals came from auctions, through dealers and from private individuals. Many people have the misconception that only old, sick or disabled animals find their way to the slaughterhouses, says Lohnes. Not so, she emphasizes. Many healthy, sound, or serviceably sound horses are presented at these plants. There is simply no one else to purchase them.

While the owner of a 1300 pound Percheron is more likely to find his horse stolen for its meat value than the owner of a Miniature Horse, Mini owners are not immune to thieves hoping to make a fast buck from horseflesh. When thieves read about five-figure prices for top quality Minis, they reason that the tiny equines will pull top dollar in the black market for exotic pets. The small size and trusting nature of Miniature Horses makes them easy prey. Mini owners in the Carolinas report thieves brazen enough to work in broad daylight in sight of the animal's owners. In one case, they succeeded in stealing a day-old foal. In another, they were foiled when the alert owner sent her Great Dane and her 192-pound Mastiff after them.

PREVENTING THEFT

Texan Amelita Donald became an AHPA activist when thieves stole two horses, a trailer and $10,000 worth of tack from the stable where she boards her mare. The two horses taken because they were the largest animals in the barn, she speculates, stood on either side of Amelita's smaller Quarter horse. Badly shaken by the crime, Amelita has become an anti-horse theft crusader helping owners trace missing horses, working for tougher legislation to protect horses on their way to slaughter, and writing articles on theft prevention.

One important step people can take to prevent their horse's theft and make it easier to locate a missing animal is to permanently mark the animal with a tattoo, brand, or microchip. A thief who knows a particular animal is traceable is more likely to move on to the next stall or pasture. If the horse is stolen, an owner has a far greater chance of finding the animal and proving ownership.

While hot branding is still seen on some horses from the Western states, most horse owners find the old cowboy practice of applying a hot iron to an animal's skin to produce a permanent scar barbaric. The practice is also of limited usefulness outside of the region where the brand was applied. Hot brands are registered by counties and unless one knows the county and state of the horse's origin, they can be hard to trace.

Associations governing racing Thoroughbreds, Arabians, and Quarter Horses have technicians at race tracks who tattoo the 2-year-olds who arrive there to begin their racing careers. *"It's not a real option for the average horse owner,"* says Gary Carpenter of the American Association of Equine Practitioners. Veterinarians do not commonly get involved with tattooing and the individual horse owner does not have access to the special equipment needed.

Michael Paulhus of the Humane Society feels that microchip identification is the wave of the future for horses. Using a long needle, a veterinarian inserts a half-inch microchip about the thickness of a pencil lead under the horse's skin. The microchip contains information such as the horse's name, registration number, and possibly even the owner's name. Once inserted, the chip cannot be seen or felt. The chip is located by using a wand that reads the information it contains.

At the moment, says Paulhus, the chief drawback to the microchip system is a lack of standardization. Different companies are promoting different and incompatible systems. Even if you know that a horse has been implanted with a microchip, there is no way of knowing which system's wand will read the chip. There is also the problem of knowing whether an animal is carrying an identification chip. Eventually, he feels, there will be national or international standards governing the implants. A lip tattoo or tiny freeze brand might identify the fact that the horse is carrying a chip. And more sophisticated chips might carry not only identification information about the horse but also the owner's name and the horse's medical history. Super chips might even give an automatic reading of the horse's pulse and blood pressure.

The most practical way of permanently identifying their horses for most owners today is freeze-marking. A supercooled iron placed against the skin destroys the hair's pigment-producing cells so that the hair turns permanently white. For light-haired horses, the iron is left in place for a longer time so that the hair follicles themselves are destroyed, leaving bare skin. in either case, what the horse feels is the same sensation his owner would feel if he squeezed a handful of ice cubes.

According to Dee Harris of Kryo Kinetics, a freeze-marking company which operates nationwide, the brand is always applied high up on the neck. While some owners like to hide the brand under the horse's mane, others prefer it to be openly visible as a theft deterrent. Recognizing that a freeze mark will grow with an animal, the company uses three different sizes of irons depending on the size and age of the animal. One iron is used for full-grown horses, another for horse foals, ponies under 13 hands and adult Miniature Horses. The smallest size is reserved for use on Miniature Horse foals.

The internationally recognized system uses angular symbols to represent letters and numbers rather than letters and numbers themselves, which could be easily altered. The symbols indicate the horse's breed (or the state where it resides if it is an unregistered animal), the horse's year of birth, and a six-digit registration number. The freeze mark is registered with Kryo Kinetics which keeps records at both its Tucson, Arizona, headquarters and another location in Arkansas in the event of fire or theft. The owner receives a copy of the freeze mark and a laminated 3" x 5" identification card that includes the owner's name and address, the name of the horse, and a drawing of the horse indicating any identifying marks such as stars, snips, whorls, scars and the like. Owners who freeze-mark their animals should also contact their breed association registry so that the mark can be noted in the horse's records. Kryo Kinetics offers a $250 reward to any person who assists in recovering a freeze-marked horse that has been legitimately reported lost or stolen.

The cost to freeze-mark an animal varies according to the distance a Kryo Kinetics technician must travel and the number of animals to be marked.

IF YOUR HORSE IS STOLEN

If a theft does occur, says Robin Lohnes, contact law enforcement officials immediately and make sure they file a report with a case number. This is the first step in the process of recovering the horse. The same day that the theft occurred, contact any nearby slaughterhouses with a complete description of the animal and, if possible, a clear photograph. Contact veterinary offices, farriers, auction houses and large dealers. If the horse is freeze-marked, notify Kryo Kinetics. The AHPA will help owners be sure that they have covered all possible avenues for recovery. If the horse is registered, also notify the registry association of the animal's theft. According to Barbara Ashby of the American Miniature Horse Association, photographs of any stolen animal immediately go up on the desks of anyone involved with new registrations. This is one reason, she points out, that AMHA requires good photographs with every horse's registration papers. If someone applies to register an animal over 24 months of age, the AMHA will check the appropriate stallion report and require blood typing to be sure the animal is as represented.

Amelita Donald emphasizes the need to keep good records on every animal you own. As she works with owners to find missing horses, she is often discouraged by their lack of solid documentation. Law enforcement officers are sometimes reluctant to become involved with cases of missing horses if they perceive that there are disputes between disgruntled lessees and lessors or between a stable owner and a boarder who have not properly documented ownership and agreements. They are simply not interested in "your version of the truth," she notes. They want proof.

Every horse should have a folder that contains the owner's bill of sale and any cancelled checks backing it up, registration papers in the owner's name, and any veterinary certificates issued on the animal, especially if they contain a physical description. Most important of all are clear photographs of the horse from all angles. The horse should fill the frame and be in good light. Take close-ups of chestnuts, whorls, scars and markings on the face or legs. Photos should be taken in both the horse's summer and winter coats or with the horse clipped and non-clipped. Remember, she says, that if your horse is recovered, his appearance may have been drastically altered by malnutrition and neglect or by grooming such as roaching the mane. People who declare they would recognize their horse anywhere sometimes express doubt when taken to a slaughterhouse to identify a particular horse.

Reprinted from Eastern Miniature, July 1992.

Besides permanently identifying animals, there are other measures recommended by AHPA personnel to protect horses from theft:

- Do not leave halters on horses, especially those at pasture. This just makes it easier for thieves.

- Make sure fences are in good repair. A stout fence may slow a thief down enough to discourage him. Also, poorly maintained fences may leave doubt in the minds of law enforcement authorities as to whether the horses were taken or wandered off on their own.

- Keep fencelines clear of brush so that all activity in a paddock is plainly visible and there is nowhere for a thief to hide. Consider changing the landscaping. Landscaping designed to provide privacy for a horse owner can also provide privacy for a thief.

- Make sure gates are securely fastened. While padlocks and keys may be a nuisance to keep track of and even a safety hazard in a real emergency, they will discourage all but the most determined thief. At a minimum, secure gates with latches that are obviously horse-proof so as to leave no doubt as to whether the horses were taken out of a pasture or let themselves out.

- Check on horses regularly, especially those that cannot be readily seen from the house or barn. While horses are creatures of routine, change the barn routine often enough that thieves cannot predict activities.

- Do not publicize your absences. When leaving town, make provision for someone to check the horses regularly throughout the day, not just at predictable feeding times.

- Avoid discussing the value of your animals in public.

- Install an alarm system and security lights. Tying the two together so that security lights go on automatically when the alarm is triggered is ideal.

- Keep a noisy dog. Flocks of noisy geese can also intimidate intruders.

SECTION 2
Keeping Your Miniature Horse Healthy

Understanding Teeth Problems in Miniature Horses
by Kenneth L. Marcella, D.V.M.

Miniature Horses have many areas where specific conditions, due either to their size or genetics, can cause medical problems. The most noticeable of these areas is that of *dentition* (teeth). Miniature Horses have a wide range of problems relating to the formation, development, eruption, and wear of their teeth. These problems then have an impact on nutrition and digestion, growth and development, and can be at the heart of a host of other problems. Let's review normal dentition in the horse and take a look at the problems that occur in Miniature Horses.

Horses, like most other species, have two sets of teeth: *deciduous*, or temporary (baby) teeth, and permanent teeth. These teeth grow out from a tooth bud, or *dental papilla*, that is located deeply imbedded in the structure of the jaw or cheek. The dental papilla produces the body of the tooth, which is then covered by enamel from cells along the edge of the tooth. Growth of the tooth is continual and it slowly erupts through the overlying gum, touches the opposing tooth and is "in-wear." Teeth are continually worn down throughout the life of the horse.

There are four tooth types in the horse. (fig. 1) The *incisors* are found in the front of the mouth and are used predominantly for grasping and tearing the food material that is funnelled into the mouth by the lips and tongue. An elephant's tusks are actually elongated incisor teeth and other incisor variations can be seen throughout the animal kingdom. The horse has three upper incisors and three lower incisors on each side of its head.

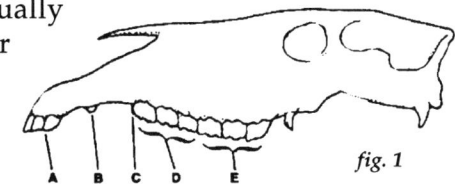

fig. 1

A—Incisors   C—Wolf Teeth   E—Molars
B—Canines (tushes)   D—Premolars

A single *canine* tooth is next seen, with one large pointed tooth visible in both the upper and lower jaw. Mares will have either absent or rudimentary canine teeth. These teeth are rarely functional from a digestion standpoint and are most likely remnants of earlier mammalian species where they may have been more prominent and had more of a function. These canine teeth are occasionally incorrectly called *"wolf teeth."* The actual wolf teeth are the upper and lower first premolars. These teeth are variable in horses, with some horses having one, two, all four, or no wolf teeth. These teeth are evident in the gum line just in front of the wider and thicker cheek teeth. Wolf teeth are important because they occupy the area of the upper gum where the bridle bit or halter strap rests when a horse is in work. These wolf teeth have a small visible crown, but can have large roots. These teeth are not always as deeply "seated" in the gum as the other molar teeth, however, and tension on the bit can be irritating and can produce a horse that is reluctant to work, unwilling to turn to one side (either toward or away from the "sore" wolf tooth), or just generally hard to train or ride. Surgical removal of these teeth is generally done prior to the horse beginning training or at whatever time a problem is noted. Because of their short crown and relatively soft attachment, these teeth are not utilized for primary chewing or grinding, and are also thought to be remnants of the mouth structure of earlier equine ancestors.

The remaining three *premolars* and three *molars* are wide, thick teeth with very large roots that go deep into the jaw and upper cheek. These teeth are predominantly used to crush and grind foodstuffs. The *occlusal surface,* or contact surface, of these molars has specific irregularities in it that make it an easier surface for grinding. These irregularities, coupled with the tight hinge of the *temporomandibular joint* (jaw hinge), make it difficult to impossible for the horse to have much lateral chewing motion. Compare this to a cow who has a much looser temporomandibular joint connection. We have all seen cows "chewing their cud." We've watched their lower jaw move laterally as they used their molars to grind their food. The horse, however, has to use less of a lateral motion and this tightly-hinged jaw leads to problems with growth and wear.

The normal horse also has a much wider upper jaw than lower jaw. This means that there is incomplete contact between the upper and lower teeth. Because these teeth cannot wear each other down evenly over time, the normal pattern of tooth growth leads to the formation of angled surfaces. The upper teeth form an angle to the outside, while the lower teeth are angled by wear to the inside. (fig. 2) These angles can become severe and the points and edges created can be sharp enough to damage other structures in the mouth. The sharp outside angles of the upper teeth can cut or abrade the cheeks and the sharp lower inside angles can abrade the tongue. The primary purpose of "floating," or filing, teeth is to maintain the proper relationship between these angles.

FLOATING TEETH

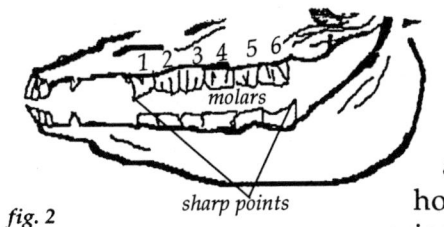

fig. 2 — molars, sharp points

Floating teeth is the main procedure done to ensure controlled wear of the teeth and to establish proper architecture in the mouth. Young horses with rapidly developing teeth may occasionally need floating, but it is the older horse with uneven tooth contact that should be evaluated for tooth wear on a yearly basis, and more often in some situations. Young horses (2-3 year olds) should be examined if there are any problems with chewing or if any drastic set-backs in training are encountered, because this is the time when horses lose their temporary teeth as the permanent teeth push up from the gum below. Occasionally, however, the temporary tooth does not release from the gum and a "retained cap" is produced. This tooth retention can be irritating or painful to the horse, and veterinary attention is needed to loosen and remove the temporary tooth.

THE ROLE OF GENETICS IN TEETH PROBLEMS

Miniature Horses can also have variations in jaw development that lead to more major dental malformations. One of the first areas to show the effects of genetic linebreeding and in-breeding is the head and jaws. Breeding closely-related canines will produce a higher percentage of genetic malformations because the genetic defects are essentially magnified. This is a double-edged sword, since in-breeding can also intensify positive genetic traits, as well. In-breeding in Thoroughbreds can help to produce a horse with more speed than either parent as easily as it can produce a foal with malformed legs or teeth or heart. Miniature Horses suffer from a limited genetic pool. Even more so than Thoroughbreds, which claim a common ancestry shared with a limited number of early stallions, Miniatures are all still fairly closely related and any mating is likely to be doubling up on some closely-related genes. Close breeding in bulldogs will produce a higher number of improper "bites" where the upper or lower jaw is malformed. This same tendency has been noted in Miniatures and some bloodlines have a higher frequency of mouth problems than others.

Breeding too closely has also been linked to other malformations of the jaws and face, which tend to produce Miniatures that have larger, more rounded heads and disproportionate bodies—or dwarfs. These horses are not balanced or properly formed, though the deviation can be difficult to see. It is imperative that these horses be recognized for what they are and the resultant information used in the formation of breeding decisions. Miniatures were originally produced by risky in-breeding, breeding the smallest to the smallest. The trait selected for was size and other problem traits were carried along as well. This is the double-edged sword of which I spoke. Now, we often have to deal with the problems that result because of the genetics used to develop the breed in the first place. No one knows if Miniatures may be reproductively less fertile or immunologically less competent because of these inbred genetic weaknesses.

We do know, however, that genetic defects occur in the facial and jaw structures. *Parrot mouth* is the most common malformation seen. (fig. 3) This defect, also called *Brachygnathism*, is a shortening of the lower jaw so that the top incisor teeth project out over the lower incisors. This defect is believed to be inherited in ponies and, though no data is available, also in Miniatures. *Prognathism*, or *monkey mouth*, (fig. 4) where the upper jaw is shorter and the lower jaw projects out below the upper incisors is also seen and is inherited in some Highland and Welsh Pony lines. Again, note that selection for small size seems to increase the percentage of these mouth malformations.

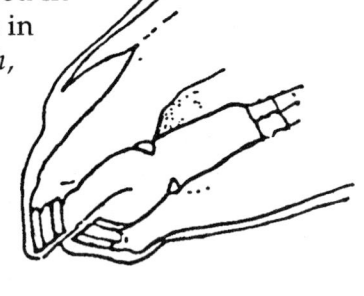

fig. 3

Both of these conditions can vary from mild to severe, and the effect that they have upon the horse varies as well. Most horses in a pasture situation can learn to graze normally even with moderately-severe parrot mouth or monkey mouth. Occasionally, horses are unable to eat enough and will be thin, smaller, and unthrifty unless supplemented with easily-consumed pellets or grain. The real problem with these malformations is that, now along with a side-to-side natural angulation of the growing teeth, these horses have a severe front to-back angulation problem.

fig. 4

For instance, in a parrot-mouthed horse, the lower jaw is shorter—meaning that the upper and lower molars will not match up or align.

The upper front molar will have no corresponding tooth below to help it wear down. Consequently, a large amount of tooth growth or "a point" will grow down in front of the lower molars. Conversely, the last lower molar will have no tooth above it to wear it down, so a corresponding point will grow up in that area. These front and back points can grow large enough to effectively lock the jaws in position and make it impossible for the horse to grind and process its food. Grain then begins to pass through these horses without being crushed and ground, which drastically decreases utilization. These horses become thin, have rough hair coats, and are unthrifty despite good appetites and hefty feed bills. Colic can be more prevalent in these horses as well, because they are trying to digest and pass large particles of food through a digestive tract that is not accustomed to such material. An easy way to spot horses with major teeth problems is to look at the manure. If you are seeing large amounts of uncracked oats or corn coming through that horse—then it's time to check the teeth!

PREVENTION AND MAINTENANCE

The key to avoiding teeth problems in Miniatures is in good prevention and maintenance. Avoid breedings that you know have produced horses with dental problems or malformations. And if such a problem does occur, act quickly. Recent advances in equine orofacial surgery have led to a number of techniques which can help these horses. If the lower first molar is surgically wired to the incisors in a foal with a parrot-mouthed conformation, the normal growth of the incisors will pull the lower jaw out and some remarkable changes in contact surfaces have been reported. There are a wide variety of such surgical procedures and more and more equine surgeons with the skill and experience needed to perform them, so that these malformations can be helped significantly.

This brings up an important ethical and moral point, however. Certainly, these "cosmetic" surgeries are warranted for that individual horse because it greatly improves its quality of life. But should that horse be allowed to breed or to be even sold without the new owner being informed that corrective, reconstructive surgery was performed to create a jaw and mouth that may now look absolutely normal? And how would such rulings or requirements be enforced?

It is considered to be veterinary malpractice to surgically implant *prosthetic* devices (artificial parts) that would make a castrated horse appear to have normal testicles, or to remove white patches on skin for the purpose of then being able to register a horse with certain breed registries, so there are precedents set. It will soon be more of a real question as our veterinary skills allow us to correct more and more of these malformations, and Miniatures Horses will be in the thick of the controversy.

Aside from surgical considerations, management of Miniatures with dental problems is the next most crucial point. An early exam to determine the degree of *malocclusion* and the areas of potential trouble will allow the owner and veterinarian to set up a floating schedule. Teeth should be checked regularly and most owners can be taught to do this. When problems are noted, then quick attention can be sought. Several companies now produce dental floats and equipment for Miniatures, and their use should be encouraged. Because of the large size of teeth and the relatively small size of the mouth of Miniature Horses, even normally formed horses will need this type of close attention.

Although it has always been said that one should never look a gift horse in the mouth (referring to checking its age), tooth care and the management of dental problems is one situation where the more you look and check, the better care you'll be able to take of your Minis.

Reprinted from Eastern Miniature, November 1991.

Understanding Basic Foot Structure
by Michael Berluti

How the horse's foot functions is of great importance. When a horse is standing, the weight carried by each forefoot is approximately one-quarter of the body weight of the horse. This is a large proportion of weight that the hoof must withstand. If we analyze the horse at the trot, the weight carried by the same forefoot is approximately one-half the horse's body weight and, at certain phases of the canter, the entire body weight is supported by one foot. This is proof that the hoof is the most important part of the horse—hence the saying, "*No foot, no horse.*"

In order for the horse owner to understand the various problems of lameness that can occur in the foot and their treatment, it is important to have a clear understanding of the basic anatomy of the foot. This would include the foot structure, location, and function of each part. Having this knowledge will enable the owner to better understand the role of the farrier and veterinarian in maintenance and treatment of the horse's feet.

The forefeet and hind feet have two distinct patterns, the forefeet being rounder and steeper than the hind feet. The function of the rounded toe is to enable the foot to *break-over*[1] easier and to travel straight. The forefeet also absorb most of the concussion from the horse's movement. The hind feet are narrower and more pointed than the front and they act as a power source. In both cases, the sole of the foot should be somewhat concave and the frog should be level with the ground at the heel.

The four major structures of the foot are the **bones, elastic structures, sensitive structures** and **non-sensitive structures**.

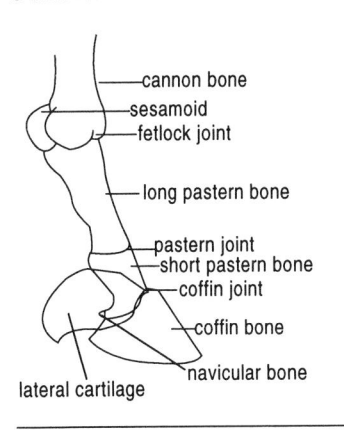

BONES

- cannon bone
- sesamoid
- fetlock joint
- long pastern bone
- pastern joint
- short pastern bone
- coffin joint
- coffin bone
- navicular bone
- lateral cartilage

The bones consist of the *coffin bone, navicular bone,* and the *short pastern bone.*

The **coffin bone** is the most important bone in the foot. It serves as a surface for attachment of blood vessels and nerves, and also as a point of attachment for the deep flexor and main extensor tendons which cause movement of the leg. The coffin bone is completely encased within the hoof.

The **navicular bone** is located between the coffin bone and underneath the short pastern bone. This bone functions as a *fulcrum point*[2] for the deep flexor tendon, which passes directly underneath it and attaches to the coffin bone.

The **short pastern bone** is located between the *long pastern bone* and the coffin bone. Only about one-half of it is encased by the hoof.

ELASTIC STRUCTURES

The elastic structures include the *lateral cartilage*, the *digital or plantar cushion* and the *coronary cushion* which function to reduce concussion. These structures also cause the hoof to expand and contract at the heel, which is necessary so that blood can be pumped from the foot back to the heart. This blood-pumping action is critical since there are no muscles in the hoof to aid in the return of blood to the heart.

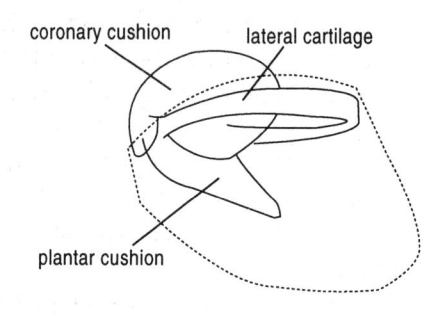

The **lateral cartilage** are located on both sides of the coffin bone. Approximately one-half of the cartilage is within the hoof and the other half is located above the coronary band.

The **digital cushion** is located between the lateral cartilage on the sides, the navicular bone on the top, and the frog underneath. The **coronary cushion** is the elastic portion of the coronary band.

SENSITIVE STRUCTURES

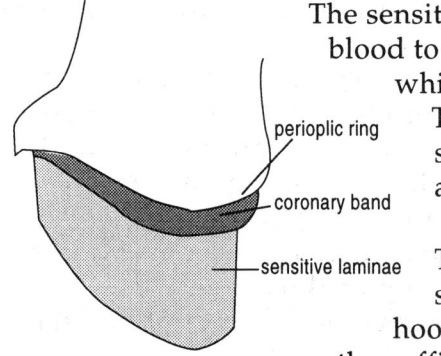

The sensitive structures in the foot carry blood to nourish and produce horny hoof, which is the cause of new hoof growth. These structures, like the elastic structures, also act as a blood pump and hydraulic cushion.

The **sensitive laminae** are leaf-like structures which lie between the hoofwall and the coffin bone, and cover the coffin bone's outer surface. The sensitive laminae are attached to the hoof wall by interlocking with the leaf-like non-sensitive laminae of the hoof wall. The coffin bone is attached to the hoof wall by this union of sensitive and non-sensitive laminae. This attachment suspends and supports nearly the entire weight of the horse at a point during the support phase of the stride. When this attachment is damaged, the horse has a disease known as *laminitis*.

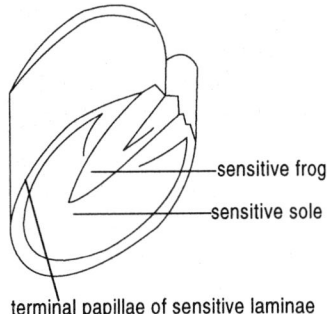

These sensitive laminae also contain various blood vessel networks of the foot. When the foot bears weight, these blood vessels are compressed between the horny wall and the coffin bone. Blood is pumped back up the leg and the remaining blood in the foot is locked inside the foot, forming a hydraulic cushion between the coffin bone and the horny wall.

The **coronary band** is located around the top of the hoof wall. Its primary function is to serve as the growth and nutritional source for the hoofwall. A severe injury to the coronary band will sometimes result in a permanent defect of the hoofwall. Some vertical hoof cracks that are always present have their origin at the coronary band.

The **periople ring** is located just above the coronary band and produces the **periople**, which aids in retaining moisture in the foot.

The **sensitive sole** covers the bottom of the coffin bone and nourishes the cells that produce the *horny sole*.

The **sensitive frog** nourishes the *horny frog*.

NON-SENSITIVE STRUCTURES

The non-sensitive structures include the *hoof wall, periople, white line, horny sole,* and the *horny frog*. These non-sensitive structures are the ones that can be seen.

The **hoof wall** is the non-sensitive horny capsule that encompasses and protects the foot, which actually consists of the sensitive structures within. The hoofwall's function is to bear weight and it is made up of three layers. The first layer consists of the *periople* and the *stratum tectorium*.

Keeping Your Miniature Horse Healthy

The **periople** on a full-size horse is a band about three-quarters of an inch wide, just below the *coronary band*.

The **stratum tectorium** is below the periople and continues down to the bottom of the foot. It is a thin layer of horny scales that gives the hoof its glossy appearance and protects it against evaporation. The next layer is the bulk of the hoof wall and is the portion that contains pigment in darker feet. The third, or inner layer, is the *laminar layer* that attaches to the sensitive laminae. The hoof wall is thickest at the toe and thinnest at the heel.

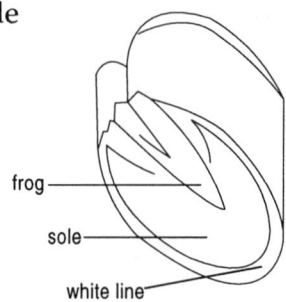

The wall grows about one-quarter to one-half inch per month. Under ideal conditions, the horse is said to grow a foot from coronary band to ground surface every twelve months. The hoof wall may grow slower in cold weather, cold climates, and even in dry weather, due to lack of moisture.

The **white line** is an irregular line around the hoof wall on the bottom of the foot. It is approximately one-eighth inch thick on a full-size horse and connects the horny sole with the horny wall.

The **horny sole** is located at the bottom of the foot and protects the sensitive sole and other parts above it. It is not designed to bear weight, so should be slightly concave and not bear constant pressure directly on the ground. This concave shape also aids in traction.

The **horny frog** is different from the other hoof structures because it is more elastic and does not turn completely into hard horn. The frog serves as a shock absorber, traction device, and circulation aid. A healthy frog, with the consistency of a rubber eraser, generally means a healthy foot. The frog should be picked clean regularly and trimmed periodically. A frog which is not trimmed will shed occasionally, but this is rarely observed except with neglected horses.

To enable the foot to expand and contract properly, and work efficiently, the foot must maintain proper elasticity. The moisture content of the hoof greatly affects this elasticity. The frog is the most elastic and the hoof is the least elastic. There is constant evaporation taking place from the hoof and, therefore, moisture must be replaced regularly to compensate for this loss.

Horses in dry climates, such as west Texas, have extremely hard soles and frogs because of this lack of moisture. Horses from the Northwest coastal area have softer and more malleable soles and frogs. Thus, moisture content can vary as a result of season, climate, nutrition, disease or genetics. To ensure proper function of the various structures of the horse's foot, regular maintenance by a professional farrier is necessary. This maintenance, if performed properly, will provide correct weight distribution on the hoof wall, arrest the formation of chips and cracks, aid in the treatment and eradication of *thrush*[3], and provide proper angling, which is essential to the quality and ease of movement.

Reprinted from Eastern Miniature, March 1991.

---

1 *the distance from the point of the heel as it leaves the ground to the toe where it leaves the ground.*
2 *the structural point that is the point of lift or movement.*
3 *an infection caused by lack of proper cleanliness of the hoof and prolonged contact with wet bedding. A foul-smelling, blackish discharge from the frog is a sign of this disease.*

SECTION 3
Breeding and Raising Your Own

How Your Mare Reproduces
by Kenneth L. Marcella, D.V.M

Every spring heralds new life, and foaling season is one of the most exciting times in a horse owner's life. I want to discuss some aspects of foaling, breeding, and other topics that will, hopefully, help you to get healthier babies on the ground and more of your mares safely back in foal. In order to do that, though, a good review of equine reproductive physiology is needed. Do not let the sound of that scare you. Be prepared for a few graphs and some new terms, but if we take it step by step you will have a better appreciation for your mare's reproductive capabilities and you should have a better ability to make decisions that will optimize those capabilities. Fertility problems are relatively common in horses, and perhaps even more so in Miniature Horses. Our attempts to diagnose and treat these problems require a firm understanding of how a mare works reproductively, beyond the usual knowledge of signs of heat and cycle length. Still, the best place to start is at the beginning: so, we'll begin with the estrous cycle.

The normal estrous cycle in the mare lasts from 21 to 22 days. **Estrus**, or heat, as it is commonly called, (which is different from *estrous*), is the period in the cycle when the mare displays behavioral signs of receptivity to the stallion. Mares in estrus will be attentive to a stallion, will lift their tails, urinate frequently, contract and relax the vulva (called *"winking"*), and may even rub or bump the sides of their stalls. This part of the cycle lasts from five to seven days, but can be quite variable. **Diestrus**, the period when the mare will not accept a stallion, lasts 14 to 15 days.

Estrus is the follicular phase of the cycle because, during this time, follicles are developing within the mare's ovaries. Follicles are small fluid-filled structures that develop to produce a hormone called **estradiol** and the **ovum** (egg). Estradiol is the equine hormone of sexual receptivity and is needed for the mare to display the appropriate sexual behavior to the stallion.

Approximately 24 to 48 hours before the end of estrus, the follicle ruptures and releases an egg. The release of an egg is called **ovulation** and this egg is then passed on to the uterus for conception. The ruptured follicle is filled in with blood and then specific **luteal tissue**. This filled in structure is now called a **Corpus Luteum** (or CL) The CL then begins to produce the hormone **progesterone.** This hormone causes the mare to reject the stallion at this stage of the reproductive cycle. This hormone is very important to the reproductive functioning of the horse, and alterations in progesterone levels may well be involved with infertility, abortion, and other such problems.

The equine estrous cycle is controlled by hormones produced initially in the *pituitary gland* in the brain. These hormones travel to the ovaries via the bloodstream and there is mounting evidence that other parts of the brain, as well as the external environment (temperature, light, weather, stress), exercise some control over the estrous cycle. The *pineal gland* in the horse's brain senses the amount of daylight through a nervous system connection with the eyes. This gland produces a hormone that exerts a depressive effect on the function of the ovaries. The rate of production and release of this hormone is inversely proportional to the amount of light received by the horses—more light, the less hormone released and the more active the ovaries are. In the natural state, this guarantees that horses are reproductively most active in the months of May, June, and July when the day length and amount of natural light is greatest. This also guarantees that most foals will be born in June, July, and August

SPRING *fig. 1*

↑ Temperature
↑ Daylight
↑ Nutrition
↓
Secretion of GnRH by Hypothalmus
↓
Secretion of FSH
↓
Growth of Follicle
↓
Secretion of LH
↓
Ovulation
↓
Formation of a CL
↓
Progesterone Secretion
↓
Pregnancy
↓
Uterine Production of Progesterone
↓
Maintenance of Pregnancy and Normal Delivery

↓ Progesterone
↑
Regression of CL
↑
Increase PGF2 alpha
↑
No Pregnancy

A simple illustration showing the cyclical nature of reproduction in the normal mare.

when temperatures are mild and when grass should be plentiful. The low level of light in the late fall and winter months produces a high level of this regulating hormone and, generally, the ovaries of mares "shut down" or become inactive during this time. (fig. 1)

This is the first situation where a knowledge of the mare's reproductive physiology can have a positive effect on your breeding program. It has been shown that increasing the amount of light that mares are exposed to during the winter months will cause shedding of the winter coat within 60 to 90 days and will initiate ovarian activity with functional ovulation within 30 to 60 days. Practically, what this means is that artificial light started in late November (or early December in the northern hemisphere) will produce a breeding season that will begin in February. This early breeding season corresponds to the artificially imposed birth date of January First as the birth date of most breeds. This imposed birth date does not apply to Miniature Horses; the actual foaling date is the date used for registration and calculation of age. The same thing could be accomplished—and reproductive fertility even more greatly enhanced—by simply moving the birth date to June First. The bureaucratic problems associated with such a change have proven almost insurmountable, so it is current practice to use automatic timers and one 200-watt incandescent or two 40-watt fluorescent bulbs for a standard box stall. Light can be increased by 30 minutes per week, or started at the maximum amount of 15-16 hours daily. Either method seems to produce the same results. The month of December averages 8-10 hours of daylight, so an additional 6 hours need to be added. Most horse owners start this artificial lighting on Thanksgiving Day to insure breeding by the early part of February. Miniature Horses are not raced and the large size so highly prized in other breeds for athletic competition and halter classes is unimportant in Miniatures. The only reason for early breeding in Miniature Horses, therefore, is to get problem mares cycling earlier in order to be able to treat them and, hopefully, get them ready to conceive later in the breeding season.

ENTER: THE HORMONES

The increasing light provided to these mares decreases the production of hormone by the pineal gland. The light also stimulates another area of the brain, the *hypothalmus*, to produce GnRH. GnRH is called **Gonadatropin Releasing Hormone**. This hormone travels to the ovaries and stimulates the release of FSH (called **Follicle Stimulating Hormone**) and LH (**Luteinizing Hormone**). Recent research has shown that the nature of

GnRH release (high frequency or low frequency) determines which ovarian hormone is released.

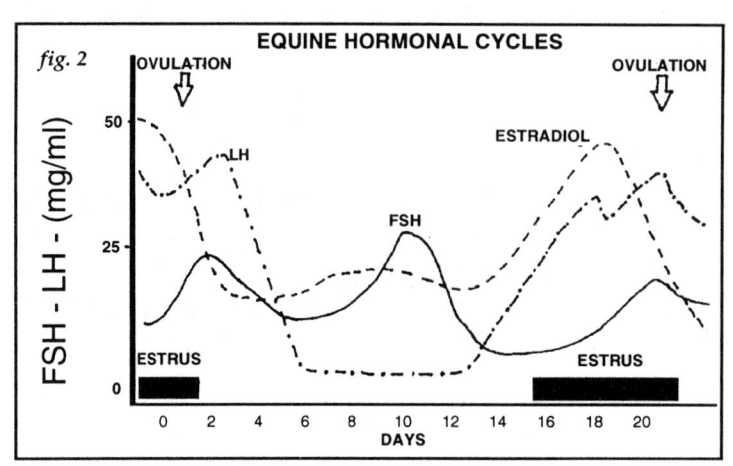

fig. 2 **EQUINE HORMONAL CYCLES**

This is where it gets confusing, so take a deep breath, pay attention, and let's go slowly!

FSH concentrations peak twice during the estrous cycle. (fig. 2) The first peak is believed to be associated with a priming effect on several small **follicles** that induces a few of these to grow further. The second peak has a similar effect on other developing follicles. This produces two "pools" of follicles that are developing at slightly different stages. The group of follicles that reaches maturity during the peak in LH levels is further stimulated by this hormone, and it is this group of follicles that eventually produces the follicle that grows large enough to ovulate, while the other follicles regress. It is the development of these dominant follicles that the veterinarian follows, either by rectal palpation alone or, preferably, by transrectal ultrasound, in order to determine the optimum day for breeding and fertilization. Follicles develop in a set pattern, which may vary from mare to mare, however, and by checking and rechecking size and firmness (soft versus hard), many useless breedings can be avoided. The standard practice in handbreeding situations is to breed, (or "*cover*") the mare every other day until she no longer accepts the stallion. But we now know that only the insemination associated closely with ovulation will be productive, and that unnecessary breedings reduce the stallion's capacity, increase chances of trauma or infection to both the stallion and the mare, and are wasted efforts in terms of time and expense. This knowledge about follicle growth also explains mares that show "*split heats*" or that double-ovulate. These mares produce two or more dominant follicles that ovulate a few days apart. This causes a mare to show estrus, breed, and then reject the stallion. She then shows heat and breeds again only a few days later. There is some speculation as to whether or not problems in follicular growth relate to the production of twins.

The large maturing follicle begins to produce estradiol, as we have mentioned. This hormone causes the mare to exhibit normal estrus behavior and assures that she will accept the stallion when she is ready to ovulate. The surge of LH at the beginning of estrus completes the follicle's development and starts ovulation. (fig. 3) The follicle grows rapidly, softens, and then ruptures, releasing the egg. The ruptured follicle fills with blood first and then becomes a CL. Within one or two days of ovulation, the CL begins to produce progesterone which terminates estrus behavior in the mare and makes the ovaries unresponsive to other hormones. The blood clot is gradually resorbed and the CL continues to produce progesterone until day 14 or 15 of the cycle. If the mare did not become pregnant on this breeding, her uterus begins to produce the hormone **Prostaglandin F2alpha** (PGF2a). This hormone affects the CL and causes it to *lyse* (degenerate). Without the presence of progesterone, the ovary is again able to respond to FSH and LH. The mare now starts to come into estrus again as follicles begin to develop. This cycle continues over and over again until the mare becomes pregnant, or until decreasing daylight produces enough regulating hormone to make the ovaries unresponsive to LH and FSH, and activity ceases for the winter.

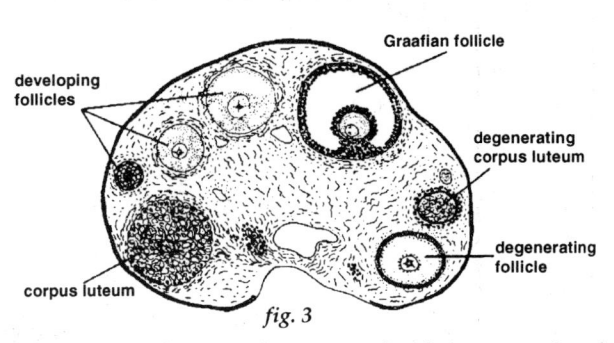

Cross-section drawing of an ovary, showing a composite of follicular activity throughout the estrous cycle.

Now, pat yourself on the back if you are still reading. With the basics of the mare's physiology understood, we can look at the practical and clinical applications of our knowledge.

GETTING THE MARE IN FOAL

When a mare begins to cycle in the spring, or earlier under the influence of artificial lighting, the concentration of FSH begins to increase, but in an irregular pattern. As the mare progresses into more regular cycles, the normal double (*biphasic*) FSH peaks appear. (fig. 2)

Practically, this means that the first few cycles exhibited by the mare will generally not be fertile because normal follicles will not be produced.

The mare may have enough FSH, LH and estradiol to cycle and exhibit estrus, but the follicles themselves are not exposed to high enough concentrations of these hormones to properly ovulate. Not understanding this fact and these early "transition" heats leads to owner dissatisfaction when mares frequently do not "*settle*" (become pregnant) early in the breeding season.

About 20% of mares can display seasonal **polyestrus**, meaning that these mares, because of individual variation, continue cycle year 'round. The percentage of polyestrous mares increases as one gets closer to the equator because of the naturally long days.

Multiple ovulations are another variation of normal mare behavior that we have mentioned. Such ovulations are undesirable because of the increased chance of twins which is commonly associated with abortions in the mare. With the arrival of ultrasound use in equine practice, however, multiple ovulations are not as much of a threat as previously, because veterinarians can now diagnose twins at an earlier stage. One of the embryos can then be manually aborted, leading to a successful pregnancy with the remaining embryo.

Silent heats can be a problem with some mares and represent times when the mare ovulates, but does not exhibit signs of estrus behavior. One study put the percentage of silent heats in 11 mares over a two year period at roughly 24%. Palpation and ultrasound can help detect these silent heats, but they still remain a problem for breeders. Hormonal stimulation is sometimes necessary to get these mares to cycle correctly and to become pregnant.

Persistent CL's are another problem that can keep mares from cycling properly. This is the most common cause in horses for a mare's failure to cycle, except, of course, for pregnancy. A persistent CL results when a mare's uterus does not produce sufficient prostaglandin to destroy the CL, which, in turn, continues to produce progesterone which keeps the mare from cycling. Standard treatment in such cases is to inject the mare with synthetic PGF2a. This causes a degeneration of the CL and a return to estrus, for most mares, in two to four days. Additionally, PGF2a is used to "*short cycle*" a mare. If a mare has ovulated before she could be presented to the stallion, or for whatever reason, she has not been bred on this cycle, she can be brought back to a point of receptivity earlier than the standard 21 days by using a timed dose of PGF2a. By giving a mare a dose of PGF2a at Day 6 or 7 after ovulation, the CL will be removed earlier and the follicles will be allowed to develop more quickly. The mare will return to estrus in two to five days and will ovulate six to twelve days after the injection. This shortened cycle can also help mares that have to be treated for a uterine infection because they can be re-bred earlier without losing valuable breeding time. The other major use for PGF2a is for induced abortions in mares before Day 35 of gestation. A single dose during this period aborts the fetus without other harmful effects.

Normally, PGF2a is produced by the lining of the uterus as a signal to the ovaries that the mare is not pregnant and that the next cycle should begin. If the mare is pregnant, however, no such signal is sent and the ovarian CL produces progesterone, which acts on the cervix and the uterus to maintain pregnancy. Structures that appear on the uterine lining during pregnancy begin to produce progesterone at approximately 70 to 90 days of gestation. After that point, the ovaries and the CL are no longer needed to maintain pregnancy. In fact, mares have had their ovaries removed after Day 120 of gestation and have carried the fetus to term and delivered normally. Currently, many mares who have had problems with past abortions are put on supplemental progesterone therapy. *Regumate®* is given to these mares daily beginning soon after conception and continuing to 150 days in most mares. There is substantial controversy surrounding these practices, in that there is no clear-cut evidence that true progesterone deficiency exists as a cause of abortion in the mare. Blood samples taken after conception that show a concentration of less than 4.0 ng/ml. of progesterone are thought to indicate a mare at risk, and supplementation has helped mares which have previously aborted early in gestation. Some researchers claim, however, that it is problems with PGF2a release that causes early abortion and, clearly, more work needs to be done. It is difficult to correctly advise owners and there are as many individual beliefs and regimes as there are veterinarians and farm managers.

Synthetic progesterone supplementation can be used to great advantage, however, in the early breeding season to eliminate the early erratic heats and to produce a breedable estrus at an earlier date. If prostaglandin is given daily to a mare in early spring, it serves to stop the cycle, much as a CL would do. This gives the hypothalmus and ovaries time to "catch up" and to coordinate hormonally. Then, when the prostaglandin is stopped, the follicles can react to the now-efficient levels of FSH and LH, and a functional estrus can result. This hormonal manipulation will work only if the ovaries are producing follicles of sufficient size. Thus, palpation and ultrasonography must be done first to confirm that the mare will respond. If no such follicles exist, then one must allow the mare time and light until she is ready to respond.

Synthetic progesterone has also found a use in effectively keeping a mare out of estrus while on the show circuit. Some mares have behavioral changes associated with estrus that makes them unshowable and unusable during this time. Daily administration of progesterone will keep the mare from coming into heat until the drug is stopped. At that time, the mare will start to exhibit estrus, but hopefully, it will now be at a time when she will not be expected to perform.

Another hormone that we must mention is **Human Chorionic Gonadatropin**, or HCG. This human hormone has been shown to help induce ovulation in the horse when given to a mare with a large mature and soft follicle. A dose of HCG given at the proper time will cause ovulation in 24 to 48 hours and has become frequently used in artificial insemination procedures (not allowed by the Miniature Horse registries) and in hand-breeding with some mares.

This has been a large volume of technical information regarding all the things that have to progress correctly in order for a mare to cycle, ovulate, conceive, and maintain her pregnancy until she delivers your long-awaited foal. And believe me, we have just scratched the surface of reproductive physiology. You should also now have an idea of all the possible points where things can go wrong. We are beginning to take more and more control of natural processes and it is our knowledge of these processes that allows us to do this. Yet, with reproduction and pregnancy in mares, just because we can manipulate the cycle does not mean that there is any advantage in doing so for the vast majority of horses. Many farms that follow time-tested procedures and allow their mares to cycle and conceive as naturally as possible have excellent conception and foaling percentages. It is the subfertile or problem mare that benefits most from our expanding knowledge of reproductive physiology. The Miniature Horse mare might also be considered in this category because infertility—for a host of reasons—seems to be more of a problem in Miniatures than in full-sized horses. It is these mares and these situations, then, which require artificial control and hormonal manipulation on occasion. Hopefully, you now have a broader understanding of your mare's reproductive capabilities and the intricacies involved in this almost magical process of breeding horses. There is a lot to learn—it is definitely worth the effort and no one said that it would be easy!

Reprinted from Eastern Miniature, March 1992.

The Crystal Ball—Predicting Foaling
by Kenneth L. Marcella, D.V.M.

It is finally foaling time! You have diligently taken care of all the necessary preliminaries. You've made sure of your breeding dates and calculations, properly vaccinated your mare well in advance, prepared the foaling stall, collected iodine, enemas and other assorted items, and now you WAIT. You watch for the development of your mare's "bag," for the presence of "wax" on the ends of her nipples, and for the relaxation of her tail-head and pelvis. These are indicators of the all-so-important upcoming event. After notifying the vet, you take sleeping bag and pillow, large pot of coffee, and a Dick Francis novel and head out to the barn, confident that by morning you will be rewarded with the birth of a foal.

Well, all too often, what you end up with is plenty of sleepless nights. Your foal is either born earlier than expected and without proper preparation, born later than expected after a few days of 2-hour round-the-clock checks, or born in that 15-minute interval when you went inside to refill your coffee cup. All of this is frustrating enough, but what becomes sadly tragic is when a mare or a foal is lost because of an unobserved foaling.

THE NEED FOR OBSERVED OR ASSISTED FOALINGS

A wide variety of foaling alert devices, video cameras, sound sensing monitors, and other such aids have flooded the market giving the mare owner a more accurate way of being alerted to a foaling mare. Saving just one well-bred baby, avoiding one early life complication, and having the peace of mind that such systems provide often outweighs the costs. Miniature Horses often need assistance because of the small size of the mare's pelvis and the possibility of an oversized foal. Knowing when your mare might foal becomes extremely important with Miniatures. Additionally, as our reproductive technology and veterinary skills continue to advance, more and more older or "problem" mares are staying reproductively active. These mares have a greater chance of having difficulties and should have observed births and possible assistance. A "problem" mare is one that has had a difficult delivery previously—malpositioning, fetal oversize, premature placental separation, or problems with the foal standing, nursing, and being accepted by the mare. Miniature Horses frequently fall into this category as well. The need for a safe, reliable, easy means of predicting foaling is becoming more and more critical.

METHODS FOR PREDICTING FOALING TIME

There are a number of veterinary researchers who feel that they may have just found such a means of predicting foaling. A few years ago, research conducted in Britain and in the United States yielded field-tested kits that sample a mare's milk and give fairly-reliable estimations of approaching foaling times. These tests are based on the fact that the ionic content of a mare's milk changes dramatically as she approaches *parturition*, or delivery. Mare's milk begins to first show an increase in the amount of magnesium ions (particles of magnesium that are contained in the milk) and, as foaling draws even closer, a very sharp rise in the amount of calcium ions occurs. By using kits that test for the presence of these ions in milk, veterinarians feel that they can then predict which mares will foal within a 24-hour period. This does not totally eliminate the traditional "foal watch," but most owners can do a much better job of mare surveillance if they know that they only need to be watching for the next 24 hours.

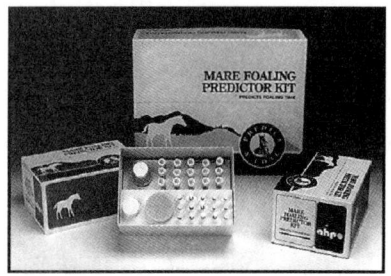

The __Predicta-A-Foal__ kit contains everything needed for performing 10 separate tests. (Photo courtesy Animal Health Products, Vernon, CA)

Not all mares follow the rules, so these tests are not 100% accurate. Tested kits, however, showed anywhere from a 60–80% chance that the mare in question would foal within 24 hours and anywhere from a 73–94% chance that the mare would not foal before reaching a particular test level. The variations noted relate to differences in the testing methods and to problems in some of the mares themselves. (Some mares will deliver premature foals and these horses will not reach the normal anticipated calcium levels before foaling. If prematurity is suspected, then other foaling detection methods, such as the FOALING MONITORING SYSTEM, should be considered; this product will be discussed later in this article.

It has been almost 6 years since the initial testing was done on the milk test kits. They have been used at many breeding farms and have proven their usefulness within limits. There are a number of kits available. The most commonly-used are PREDICT-A-FOAL mare foaling predictor kit (Animal Health Products, Vernon, California) and FOAL WATCH

TITRETS calcium hardness test strips (Chemetrics, Inc., Calverton, Virginia). Both kits are complete, with simple to follow instruction for use.

One key to accurate testing is to eliminate the presence of dirt or other contaminants which contain stray ions and confuse the results. All the pieces of your kit should be cleaned well before use, rinsed well with tap water, rinsed again with distilled water and allowed to air-dry. Rinsing with distilled water is essential, as tap water contains many ions which will alter results.

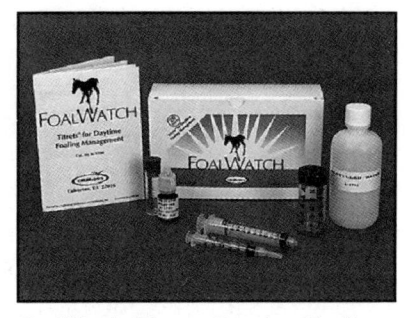

FoalWatch Titrets *Daytime Foaling Management Kit provides everything you need.* (Photo courtesy Chemetrics, Inc., Calverton, VA)

The actual testing procedure is roughly the same for each kit. Wash and rinse the mare's udder and gently milk out 2-3 cc. into a paper cup. *Sure*, you say!

True, not all mares will let you touch their nipples and some are bound to be nearly impossible. This is another good reason to begin this training early-on with your broodmares. You should gradually be getting them used to this procedure over the last trimester of pregnancy so that you can slowly work from the stifle area to the belly and finally back to the nipples. Try doing this around feeding time, using grain as a partial reward for good behavior. Since many mares that reject foals seem to be very upset with the foal's attempts at nursing, getting your mare used to being touched and milked might help avoid such a situation in the future.

COLOSTRUM—CRUCIAL TO THE NEWBORN FOAL

Avoid milking out more than is needed because this early milk contains valuable antibodies that the foal requires, and while a few cc's every other day will have no effect, refrain from taking too much. Remember that it is also a good idea to have your newborn foal checked to be sure that it has absorbed the proper amount of *colostrum*, the antibody-rich first milk. Your veterinarian can perform a simple blood test when the foal is about 24 hours old to tell you about its immune status. Foals that do not absorb enough or who have dams that produce poor quality colostrum are at risk from a host of diseases during their first weeks of life. Additional antibody protection can be given to these deficient foals if they are diagnosed early enough.

The next step is to place 6 cc. of distilled water in a clean paper cup or test tube. Add 1 cc. of mare's milk to the water and gently mix the solution. This mix can now be tested with the various test kits according to the individual directions. Some tests are easier to perform than others, but with a little practice, all are well within the capabilities of the average owner.

The individual kits will indicate how close, or far, a mare may be from foaling. A value of 250 parts per million of calcium is the level at which these kits seem to be able to be predictive. In other words, if you test your mare today and she shows *less* than 250 ppm. of calcium, these tests indicate that there is only a very small chance that the mare will foal within 24 hours. I usually recommend rechecking in two days. If you check your mare and her calcium level is *greater* than 250 ppm, she is close and the actual time to foaling depends on the specific test used and the actual calcium level recorded. Values of 500 ppm. or greater usually mean a foaling within 12 hours.

FOALING ALERT SYSTEMS

If you have a number of mares and just can't be sleeping in the barn even for one night, or you have a mare that routinely foals during the day, or you feel that you just have to be there because of a possible problem, then you may want to consider the Foaling Monitoring System (Foalert, Inc., Marietta, GA). This system consists of a small radio transmitter that is sutured to one side of the mare's vulva and a magnet that is attached to the other side of the vulva. (See fig.1) When the foal begins to come through the vulva, the fetal sac pulls the magnet out of the magnet shelf on the transmitter, which then sends a silent signal that activates the receiver. Additional functions are available through accessories. There is a secondary alarm for a nearby location, a paging system that consists of a pager and a pocket receiver, and a security autodialer that can be programed for up to three numbers. The Foaling Monitoring System works well and has caught on at many breeding farms.

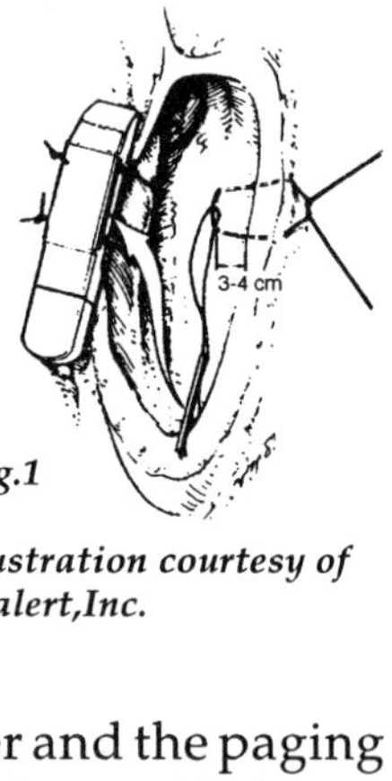

fig.1

Illustration courtesy of Foalert, Inc.

There are a few problems, though. The basic system relies on a distance of 150 feet from transmitter to receiver and the paging system accessory has a range of up to 3 miles. Some mechanical barriers such as heavy metal doors or buildings can affect the range of the basic system; hills and valleys, mountains, and heavy tree growth can affect the signal sent from the transmitter to the pocket receiver. Very heavy mares or mares with poor vulvar conformation can occasionally break the connection in the transmitter simply by lying down during late gestation. In these mares, the vulvar lips often *evert*, or extrude, when they lie down and a false alarm can result. No harm is done, however, and the transmitter can simply be reset. Some mares will rub or scrape the transmitter off their vulvas and these will have to be resutured. The system is designed to detect one physical parameter—the physical separation of the vaginal lips. It is possible for a mare to have a dystocia without having separation of the vaginal lips. (This would be something to discuss with your veterinarian, if you have mares with this type of history.) All in all, though, the Foaling Monitoring System is another viable method of predicting foaling and might be the method of choice for your personal situation. It would be a good idea to talk to other Miniature Horse owners who have used this system to ascertain whether this one is for you.

Since 345 days is a long time to wait, it is simply foolish not to try to be there at the most important point. We have already mentioned that Miniature Horses tend to have a higher share of foaling problems. As a breed, they could be greatly helped by having a greater number of assisted deliveries. The calcium test kits are so inexpensive that they make good economic sense. Even the more expensive options, such as the Foaling Monitoring System, or video cameras and sound surveillance set-ups all still seem realistic when compared with a weak foal, a lost foal, and possibly a lost broodmare. Technology and medicine are continually offering us more options and it is up to horse owners to become educated and avail themselves of these new advances. Who knows, the foal you save may be that special one you've been waiting for.

Selection for the Miniature Horse Breeder
Part I
by Toni M. Leland

Any good breeding program is based on planning and careful management. The importance of these two factors cannot be stressed enough, for without them, mediocrity is the result. The inheritance of good qualities in the offspring is the goal of the serious breeder and laying a "game plan" is the first step toward achieving that goal. A horse may pass individual good genes to his offspring, but he cannot pass his particular combination of genes. There is an element of luck involved in determining a horse's potential, but the horseman can shift the odds to his side by selecting wisely on the basis of certain predefined standards.

The Miniature Horse owner wishing to establish a breeding program must first determine the purpose that his or her horses will serve. Certain characteristics are desireable for specific jobs: show horses, performance horses, breeding stock, or the "pet market."

For show animals, the usual requirement is that the animal participate in both conformation and performance classes to prove their superior characteristics. This is a direct result of the belief that good conformation and good athletic ability signify a superior individual—one that has the potential for passing on some of these traits.

So, for selection purposes, the prospective breeder must consider what minimum characteristic standards he will accept and then carefully assess each and every individual already in his program and, obviously, any new horses he plans to integrate into the herd.

Some selection characteristics to consider are: pedigree, conformation, soundness, performance, size, color, reproductive performance, disposition, and age. As a starting point for this discussion, the pedigree and its value to the breeder will be explored. Other selection characteristics will be covered in later articles.

PEDIGREE

There is a great deal of controversy among breeders over the importance of pedigree. There are those that believe that the presence of outstanding individuals in the pedigree does not guarantee that the offspring will inherit their desirable *genotypes* (inherited gene types). It is possible for a Miniature Horse to have a champion great-grandsire and still possess none of his genes. However, researchers have related that the probability is that approximately 12% of the horse's genes will come from that outstanding stallion.

When using the pedigree as a guide to an individual horse's genetic make-up, one must consider the fact that desireable gene combinations may not pass from parent to offspring. However, the pedigree can usually be relied upon as a "road map" for hidden strengths and weaknesses in a group of ancestors. Breeders using this "map" in their search for desireable breeding stock could want either horses that have been linebred to a particular sire, which results in duplication of desirable traits, or horses bred by crosses between families. This very often results in foals that are superior to either parent. This is known as *hybrid vigor*.

Unfortunately, pedigrees are only as good as the records that were kept on the individuals involved. In Miniature Horses, this is especially important, given the uncertainty of the beginning of the breed—a very controversial subject. Stud books are maintained by the Miniature Horse registries and these offer a good starting point for research. A simple pedigree cannot reveal the performance or breeding records of ancestors and most horseman don't have the opportunity to examine the ancestors first-hand. Names alone do not predict the potential of the individual and without good tracking back, the horseman must rely more on the individual's conformation, performance, and production records.

The *heritability estimate* is the term for assessing the probability that a certain trait will be passed from parents to offspring. Traits such as jumping ability are more heritable than, say, pulling power.

For the purposes of selecting breeding stock, the advantage of a pedigree that contains information on individuals that share common ancestors, such as cousins, brothers, etc. *(collateral relatives)* is that it will point out the presence of favorable recessive genes that are hidden by less favorable dominant genes. Studying a pedigree in detail could show that an above-average horse resulted from pure luck, if his collateral relatives were just average to poor performers. Likewise, a horse of only average ability could show consistently outstanding collateral relatives in the pedigree. This horse will usually be a better breeding prospect because his many good genes may be masked by dominant genes or unfavorable gene interactions.

A horse's potential could be determined using the pedigree, as long as serious consideration is given to these areas:
1) close ancestors
2) heritability of desired traits
3) collateral relatives
4) progeny records
5) degree of inbreeding (mating of relatives)

Close Ancestors

Parents, grandparents and great-grandparents are the ancestors that have the most significance in a pedigree. Relatives past the third generation have less impact unless the horse is heavily inbred to a particular animal. In that case, descendants could have the genes of that ancestor. All breeds of horses are inbred and the Miniature Horse is no exception. Therefore, it is highly probable that there are common ancestors in the seventh generation which should not be ignored. A horse's inheritance is filtered through, making any common ancestors in the 7th generation the most important ones in his pedigree. As clues to the parents' genotypes, more distant relatives are useful. When studying a pedigree, the Miniature Horse breeder should look carefully at the horses in the first two generations. If these 6 individuals show no merit, then it is probable that the more distant ancestors can usually be ignored, even if they are superior. This shows that many of their good genes were not passed on to their foals. Consistency in a pedigree implies a high degree of heritability of the desired characteristics.

Heritability

Traits such as coat color, blood groups, sex, etc. (known as *qualitative traits*) have a heritability estimate of 100%. The reason for this is that these traits are due entirely to genetic factors. Speed, jumping ability, intelligence, etc. (known as *quantitative traits*) are influenced by the environment. These traits are considered highly heritable in the 30-40% range.

Collateral Relatives

Brothers, sisters, or cousins can help a breeder make some predictions on future performance and show any desirable recessive genes that are masked by dominants. A full brother or sister can resemble the horse because they contain about 50% of the same genes. Why only 50% instead of 100%? During cell division (*meiosis*), the parental chromosomes split and half of the cell from each parent passes on to the foal. What are the odds of the best genes from each parent being passed to the foal? Unknown—because "Chance" makes the choice. This explains why the full-sibling to your most outstanding horse may be a disappointment. Unfortunately, using exactly the same mating that produced your great horse is not a guarantee for a duplicate foal.

About 25% of a horse's genes are shared in common with his aunts and uncles. They are full brothers and sisters of his parents (50% related to his parents). Each grandparent shares about 25% of its genes in common with its second-generation descendant, because 50% of its genes were passed on to its immediate offspring which, in turn, passed on 50% of its genes to the foal. So, in looking at pedigrees, the horseman must remember that only 25% of the grandparents' genes are present in a grandson or granddaughter.

Progeny Records

If a pedigree tells what an animal *should* be and his actual performance and appearance tell what he *seems* to be, then his offspring should tell what he *actually is*. A horse's offspring (progeny) can reveal its genotype. If one stallion is bred to several different mares resulting in a diverse crop of foals to study, a breeder can determine whether or not the stallion carried the desired genes for his purposes. This is especially true if the mares' genotypes are known. Because of the time involved, this type of progeny testing is not possible with mares

BREEDING SYSTEMS

Any breeding system's success is dependent on careful analysis of the breeder's goals. Available finances, experience of the breeding manager, size of the breeding operation, and quality of the foundation stock must be considered before the Miniature Horse owner decides upon a breeding program. Many systems exist—some more risky than others, and all of them entail a financial risk. The disappointment of waiting 11 months for a foal, then having it be only mediocre, is discouraging, at best. However, the serious Miniature Horse breeder that wants to strengthen his herd and produce animals with high market value, must conscientiously practice culling in these instances.

CULLING

Culling is one of the most important techniques for breed improvement. It is the practice of eliminating undesirable animals from a breeding herd. This can be accomplished by selling them or changing the use of the animal (i.e., training an animal for pleasure driving, gelding a stud colt, etc.). If natural or artificial selection was accomplished, each generation would be a rubber stamp reproduction of their immediate ancestors. A herd would remain unchanged from generation to generation. Improvement within the breed is a direct result of culling and selecting for above average individuals. (fig. 1)

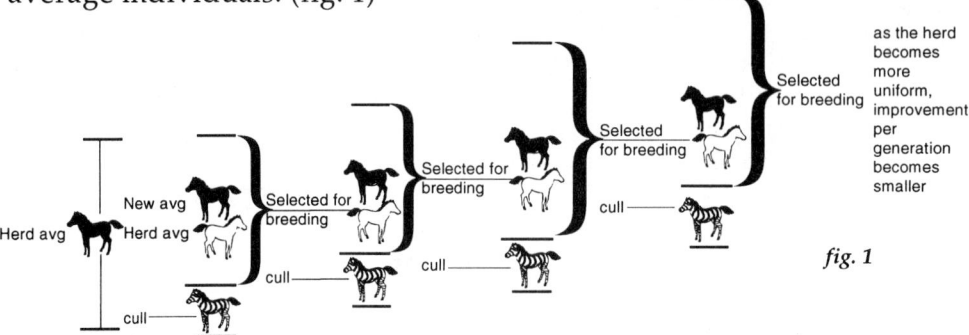

fig. 1

The overall character of a horse is influenced by both genetics and environment. Based on evaluation of genetic and environmental variation, a breeder should keep only his most outstanding foals as prospective breeders. Further evaluation of the parents of these foals must be made to determine if they have made significant contributions to his breeding program. By strictly adhering to these standards, the Miniature Horse breeder can confidently improve his breeding herd over time.

As one can see from the information given here, a good breeding program is definitely dependent upon good planning and the patience to follow the plan. The production of fine horses takes time—there are no overnight miracles. Most of the breeding systems and selection procedures outlined in this article take quite a bit of time. However, for the serious breeder of Miniature Horses, the attention to detail can pay off in a high standard of excellence and the improvement of the breed.

Reprinted from Eastern Miniature, July 1991.

Cesarean section in the Miniature Horse
Between a Rock and a Hard Place
by Kenneth L. Marcella, D.V.M.

Cesarean section is a very common surgical procedure for delivery of a fetus. It is used in humans and animals. Puppies and kittens are often delivered this way, most commonly because they are too big to fit through their mother's pelvis. In dogs, breeds with thick necks and large heads tend to encounter such problems more frequently, so more Bulldogs and Boston Terriers are delivered by C-section than Collies and Poodles, for example. This method of delivery is also very common in cattle since bulls often field-breed young cows and the resultant calves are too big to be delivered normally. Cattle tolerate the procedure so well that the surgery is often done with the cow standing up the entire time and with the calf delivered through the cow's side or flank. Horses, however, are a very different story.

THE RISKS ENTAILED WITH C-SECTION

Cesarean sections have always been only a last resort in horses because of the very fragile nature of the equine fetus. *Parturition*, or delivery, in the horse occurs in a relatively short period of time, usually about one hour. Foals that experience difficulty during the delivery process do not have very long before they begin to suffer from a lack of oxygen. Consequently, problems during delivery in the horse are either corrected very quickly or there is a risk of losing the foal and possibly the mare. C-section surgery in the horse requires general anesthesia and a surgical operating room with professional staff. Because the time available to mare owners to find a problem requiring C-section surgery and then transport the horse to a surgical hospital is almost always greater than the one hour delivery time, very few live cesarean deliveries were performed on horses. Simply put, because of the nature of delivery in horses, by the time you realize that you have a surgical emergency, it is usually too late. Add to this the exceedingly high rate of complications due to post-operative bleeding that was associated with C-section and you can see why this procedure on mares was routinely viewed as a last resort.

Every effort is made to first correct the positioning of the fetus, as this is the most common cause of *dystocia* (difficulty during delivery) requiring a cesarean section. Fetal abnormalities contribute heavily to the cases of malpositioning. *Hydrocephalus* (enlarged skull with fluid contained where brain tissue should be (Fig. 1-A), *ankylosed* (fused) joints, contracted tendons (Fig. 1-B) and a few other genetic deformities are the most common ones seen in dystocia cases. Because of the intense line-breeding of some Miniatures Horses, it is wise to closely watch the genetics of intended breedings so as to discourage the production of colts and fillies with in-bred genetic defects. Excessively large or "dwarfish" heads, small eyes, contracted tendon problems, and any behavioral abnormalities should be selected against and breeding match-ups made accordingly. Still, some genetically-normal foals will be poorly positioned and may yet need a C-section. Tears in the uterus or uterine rupture (often due to a kick or other such trauma) can be another sign that a C-section is necessary. The presentation of all four feet of a foal at the same time, or the lack of any part of the foal appearing during delivery may signal the need for a C-section. Many times, an experienced veterinarian can reposition the foal and accomplish a normal delivery, and this is the desired result. (See fig. 2) However, if normal position cannot be achieved, if a tear or rupture is suspected, or an oversize fetus or true abnormality exists, C-section in the horse should no longer be considered a last resort.

fig. 1

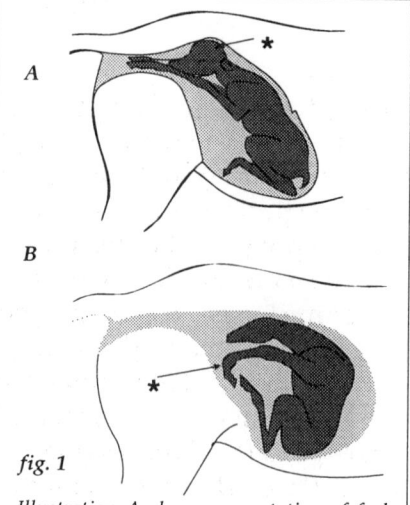

Illustration A shows presentation of foal with hydrocephalus. Illustration B shows how contracted tendons affect passage through the birth canal.

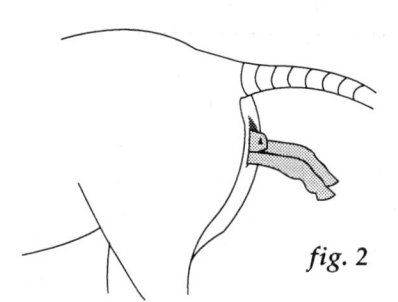

fig. 2

This illustration demonstrates the proper presentation in a normal delivery.

Improvements in anesthesia have been made which now increase the survival rate and much has been learned about the specifics of blood flow to the uterus, so that changes in surgical technique have solved the post-operative bleeding problem. C-section in the mare can now be looked at in the same light as colic surgery, joint surgery, or any other such procedure. It should be considered if you feel that you may have a mare at risk for a complicated delivery. If plans and provisions are made in advance, you may be able to avoid a serious problem.

THE CRITICAL TIME-FACTOR

If your mare begins to experience difficulty during delivery, seek veterinary assistance immediately. Your veterinarian will first try to reposition the fetus using plenty of lubricant, chains, snares, hooks, and lots of effort. If the foal cannot be repositioned and delivered during this time period, there is a good chance that the stress and lack of oxygen will be enough to kill the fetus. The focus now shifts to the mare's safety and the veterinarian will try to remove the dead fetus. A *fetotomy* is sometimes used. In this procedure, the dead foal is cut so as to remove a leg or the head, which then provides enough room for removal of the rest of the fetus. Fetotomies are routinely done in cattle, and cows seem to recover well and successfully rebreed. Horses are much more sensitive to the damage done to the walls of the uterus when the fetus is cut and pulled out. Infection and subsequent scarring of the uterus are common findings in these mares, and they generally do not breed again. If you have planned for problems ahead of time, you may be able to avoid a fetotomy and proceed to a C-section. If you have moved your mare to a location near a surgical facility for her foaling, you may yet be able to save the foal with a C-section. But time becomes the critical factor.

MAKING THE DECISION

Cesarean section does not carry the risks of the same kind of uterine damage, and though the reproductive rates of horses with C-section surgery are somewhat lower than that of the general population, they are still quite acceptable. One study reports a conception rate of 58% following cesarean section, which is almost the rate of normal mares. This same study states that rates for mare recovery, fetal survival and post-surgical fertility were greater for elective C-section than for emergency C-section. This stands to reason because elective surgery—where a decision has been made before a crisis situation exists—is usually done on a more healthy mare and fetus, and no stress or trauma has occurred. It is very difficult to decide when a C-section is needed before the actual delivery process begins. If you choose incorrectly, you risk delivering a premature foal. You risk performing an expensive surgical procedure in a situation where a perfectly normal birth may have occurred. But, if you choose correctly, you save a foal and possibly a mare as well. Repeated use of diagnostic *ultrasound* to monitor the fetal heart rate and to attempt to size the fetus and the pelvic canal may be beneficial in making decisions about elective C-section. The reproductive history of the mare is important as well, in that, if a mare has had a problem delivery previously, she very likely may have problems again, depending upon what the previous problems were.

In order to be able to even consider a C-section you must know that your mare is having problems delivering. This makes assisted foaling important and, in Miniature Horses, crucial. There are many aids available for predicting foaling and/or alerting you to the foaling process.

You may want to consider inducing foaling as well. In this case, an injection of *fenprostalene* is used to mimic the stages of labor and to induce delivery in the mare. Many precautions must be taken to insure that the mare is indeed ready to foal, and it is not a decision to be made lightly. But there are advantages to induced deliveries, especially in Miniatures. It can be done when a veterinarian is present and, ideally, where surgical help is available should a cesarean be necessary.

While we should all be concentrating on breeding genetically sound horses that should foal naturally, we must recognize that attempting to breed smaller and smaller Miniatures increases the likelihood of dystocia. Adequate pre-foaling ultrasound exams, assisted deliveries, and pre-planning for the possibility of an emergency, seem logical steps to take. Rather than being looked at as a last resort for survival, C-section surgery in the horse has developed into a useful addition to your foaling plans. Rather than a choice between a rock and a hard place, cesarean section may provide a way out of a potentially deadly situation.

SECTION 4
The Legal Side of Horse Ownership

Are You Really in Business? The I.R.S. Wants To Know!
by Attorney Margaret Anderson-Murphy

[Editor's note: As we go to press, there is a current effort by the Internal Revenue Service to substantially change some of the rules governing "horses as a business," making them more stringent. We suggest that you keep close track of these issues through your accountant or attorney.]

Despite the downturn in the national economy, horses—and especially Miniature Horses—continue to be an attractive investment. The recent growth of the Miniature Horse industry has prompted many people to purchase more of the Minis in order to become a part of the boom and realize a profit in the process. This discussion is intended to provide some basic tax considerations for people who are just starting out in the horse business. It is by no means an exhaustive review of all applicable tax laws, and a professional tax specialist should be consulted for questions on any tax-related issue.

If you have decided that you want your horses to help pay for their upkeep, you must make a commitment to this decision and stand by it. This means consistent and accurate record-keeping and a real dedication to the business that goes beyond just paying the bills. While the Internal Revenue Service does not follow a predetermined definition of a trade or business when reviewing the taxpayer's return, a trade or business has generally been characterized as an activity carried on for a livelihood or for profit. Although a love for and enjoyment of horses may be a motivational factor for getting involved with them, such involvement will not be considered to be a business if that is the sole motivation. To be entitled to take all of the business deductions which flow from the operation of a business, you must be able to demonstrate that you are, in fact, operating a horse business.

HORSES AND THE I.R.S.

Section 183 of the Internal Revenue Code of 1986 states that if an activity is not engaged in for profit, no deduction attributable to such activity shall be allowed. This section includes a specific reference to horse-related activities. The section provides that if the gross income derived from an activity which consists in major part of the breeding, training, showing or racing of horses exceeds the deductions attributable to such activity for at least 2 out of the prior 7 consecutive taxable years, then such activity shall be presumed to be an activity engaged in for profit. (It is interesting to note that the time frame for horse-related activities is considerably more lenient than that for other activities that must show gross income which exceeds deductions in 3 out of 5 prior tax years.) An activity consists, in major part, of the breeding, training, showing or racing of horses for a taxable year if the average of the portion of expenditures attributable to breeding, training, showing and racing of horses for the prior 3 taxable years was at least 50% of the total expenditures attributable to the activity during such period.

The presumption that a horse-related activity is engaged in for profit is, however, a rebuttable one. This means that the I.R.S. can determine, based on all of the facts and circumstances, that the activity is not engaged in for profit. In that event, no deductions arising out of such activity would be allowed. The I.R.S. is required to make its determination based on reference to objective standards, and to give greater weight to objective facts, rather than to the taxpayer's mere statement of his intent. However, under the "facts and circumstances" test, the I.R.S. may determine that the taxpayer intended to make a profit, even though there appeared to be only a small chance of making one.

In order to assist you with the setting up and conducting of your horse business, the following are some of the factors which the I.R.S. may take into account in determining whether an activity is engaged in for profit:

1. **The manner in which you carry on the activity.**
   If you maintain your books and records in a businesslike manner and keep complete and accurate records, it will help you to establish profit motive. In addition, a change in your operating methods, adoption of new techniques or abandonment of unprofitable methods may also indicate a profit motive if you can show that such changes were made with the intent to improve the profitability of the business.

2. **Your expertise or that of your advisors.**
   If you hire a trainer, professional barn manager, instructor, accountant or lawyer and follow their advice in operating your

business, the I.R.S. will consider this as an indication of your intent to realize a profit. Additionally, if you can document your own efforts to learn more about the business (such as participating in seminars, clinics or classes relating to breeding, training or a similar activity), your effort to learn more about the business may help to establish a profit motive.

3. **The time invested by you in carrying on the activity.**
You need not necessarily be involved full-time with the business in order to demonstrate that you intend to profit by it. Facts which show that you have hired a trainer or instructor to oversee your business may indicate a profit motive. Of course, if you can demonstrate that you devote much of your personal time and effort to carrying on the business, whether it be mucking stalls or showing your horses, or that you have left another job to devote your time to the horse business, your case will be strengthened.

4. **Have an expectation that the assets used in the activity may appreciate in value.**
The term "profit" encompasses an appreciation in the value of your assets, which includes your horses. While you may show no profit when your horses are unproven as show horses or breeding stock, once they have "made a name for themselves," their value will be significantly increased.

5. **Your success in carrying on other similar or dissimilar activities.**
If you have engaged in a similar activity, such as dog breeding, or any other business activity in the past, and converted that former activity from an unprofitable one to a profitable enterprise, it would indicate a successful "track record." This may indicate that you are presently engaged in a horse activity for profit, even if that activity is currently unprofitable.

6. **Your history of income or loss with respect to the activity.**
The I.R.S. is aware of the fact that a new business is likely to sustain a series of losses during its start-up phase and does not necessarily consider this to be an indication that the business is not engaged in for profit. It also realizes that losses may be sustained because of unforeseen or unfortunate circumstances which you cannot control, such as disease, theft, fire, death, or even depressed market conditions. However, if after several years in which no unforeseen disasters occur, you are still

showing a loss which you cannot satisfactorily explain, the I.R.S. may take it to mean that you are not engaged in the business for profit.

7. **The amount of occasional profits, if any, which are earned.**
The I.R.S. generally looks at the amounts of profits in relation to the amount of losses incurred as useful criteria in determining your intent. Ideally, if you can demonstrate a substantial profit, although it is only occasional, you would have a strong case for arguing that your business is engaged in for profit, especially where the aggregate losses are comparatively small.

8. **Your financial status.**
This relates back to Number 3, in that if you cannot show any substantial income or capital from sources other than your business, it is a strong indication that you are engaged in your horse business for profit. If, however, you derive substantial income from other sources, the activity may not be considered a business. Particularly in conjunction with this factor, the I.R.S. looks at the personal and recreational elements involved in the activity, which are often present in a horse business.

9. **Elements in the "only activity of personal pleasure or recreation."**
As noted earlier, it is important that you be able to demonstrate that you have a motive other than personal pleasure in running your business. As long as you can demonstrate that there are other factors which support your claim that you are engaging in an activity for profit, the presence of personal satisfaction in your activity will not negate the business motive.

Again, it should be emphasized that these are only some of the factors which the I.R.S. will consider. Each taxpayer's case is different. However, these factors should provide meaningful guidelines. In addition to maintaining accurate and complete books and records, it is also a good idea to prepare and implement a well-thought-out business plan, which is updated periodically as necessary. Obviously, the more complete such a document is, the better a reference it will be for you in planning both long-term and short-term goals for your business. It will also be a strong piece of evidence in your favor should the I.R.S. question the nature of your activity. Some of the issues to be addressed in your business plan should include a description of the business itself with all relevant information as to the competition (i.e., the location of the nearest

Miniature Horse farm), financial data including sources and applications of funding, and a balance sheet, to name a few items. For an existing business, historical financial reports, tax returns, and balance sheets for the past several years should also be included. Finally, all supporting documents, such as horse registration documents, employee resumés, and legal documents should be included with the plan.

If you are just starting out in the horse business, you should be aware of the fact that you can request that the I.R.S. postpone a determination of whether your business is an activity engaged in for profit until after the close of the sixth taxable year following the tax year in which you first started your business. With some restrictions, you may elect to postpone a determination regarding the presumption of profitability within 3 years after the due date of your return for the first tax year in which you began operating your business. This is obviously a question of business judgment that you will want to discuss with your accountant.

Whether you are starting up a business or have been involved in the horse business for a number of years, for tax purposes, it is a good idea to periodically review the manner in which you conduct your business.

KEEPING GOOD RECORDS

Good record keeping is clearly essential. Aside from documentation for major purchases such as a trailer or fencing, save receipts and keep track of items such as gas for driving to and from shows, entry fees, costs of advertising your horses for sale or breeding, dues paid to associations such as the American Miniature Horse Association or Registry and state clubs, and other expenses which arise in the course of your business. Assuming that you are, in fact, conducting a business for profit, these expenses may be deducted as "ordinary and necessary" business expenses.

The more documentation you have, the better off you will be in the long run. If your record keeping in the past has been less than complete, it is not too late to start keeping accurate records for the current year, so that your next filing will be that much easier. Once your paperwork is in order, you will be able to spend more time with the real reason you went into this business—your Miniature Horses!

Reprinted from Eastern Miniature, March 1992.

Transporting Your Minis—Are You Covered?
by Attorney Margaret Anderson-Murphy

The church that I attend has recently adopted the tradition of having a small donkey participate in the Palm Sunday choir procession. Over the years, *"Peabody"* has arrived at the church in style by way of a race-car trailer or a church van which is normally used to transport worshippers on Sunday mornings. Aside from the mess the donkey made in the church van, and the lack of proper ventilation in the race-car trailer, there are other serious concerns which arise from this type of transportation of a small equine; namely, that of liability in the event of an accident.

In making preparations for your horse shows, don't forget to examine your insurance policies. That's right. I said insurance policies. In a previous article, I reviewed the various types of insurance available for horses, including mortality insurance which will, in most cases, cover your horse if it is injured during transportation. If you have mortality insurance coverage for your horses, they will be protected in an accident; but, you should not stop there.

The two types of transportation used for *"Peabody"* provide good examples of what you should consider when transporting your Miniature Horses. The race-car trailer in which the donkey arrived one year was a two-axle enclosed wooden trailer designed to house a small race car and to be towed by a standard hitch on a passenger automobile or light pickup truck. The owner of the car used it for personal use and it was, presumably, covered by a non-commercial automobile liability insurance policy. Depending on the particular policy issued to that driver, there may have been a *"trailer exclusion"* in effect which would not provide coverage for any vehicle, equipment, or other device which was pulled or towed along the road by an insured automobile. As a result, any damages caused by that trailer would not be covered by insurance. In addition to, or instead of this exclusion, such a policy may contain a

photo: Cheryl A. Lekstrom

sentence which states that there will be no coverage extended for any car which is damaged or in an accident while towing a trailer. Furthermore, the animal in the trailer will probably not be covered pursuant to the *"care, custody, & control"* exclusion, which means that the insurance company will not pay for any damage to property owned or transported by the insured or in the care, custody or control of the insured. As a result, the owner of the car may be potentially liable to the farm that owns the donkey for any injuries it sustains.

If you transport your Minis in a similar type car/trailer arrangement, you should carefully review your automobile policy. See whether it covers a trailer in the event that your car/trailer combination is involved in an accident. Keep in mind that it is possible to avoid liability problems with a trailer by adding what is known as a *"trailer endorsement,"* which will provide liability insurance for damage done by your trailer. Such an endorsement may include a specific definition of what a trailer is (or is not); so, certain types of trailers may not be covered. Obviously, you will want to make sure that the trailer in which you are transporting your horses is a covered vehicle under your policy.

While your automobile insurance policy may not specifically provide coverage for trailers, the mere fact that the policy does not describe a trailer as an insured vehicle in so many words may not exclude the vehicle from the policy's coverage, if it is clear from reading the policy that it was intended to cover the trailer. However, keep in mind that even if the trailer is insured, either by an endorsement or through the terms of the actual automobile policy, it may not be covered if you borrow the trailer from the insured owner and use it with your own vehicle. Conversely, while your policy may exclude trailers which are owned or rented by you, the policy may extend coverage to a trailer which is simply lent to you by another person.

Given the state of the law with regard to vehicles which pull trailers, it is especially important to make sure that the trailer you are pulling is covered by insurance. Generally, although the state laws may vary somewhat, the owner of a motor vehicle to which a trailer is attached is held liable for any loss or injury which is caused by a defect in the trailer fastening or hitch which causes the trailer to break loose from the towing vehicle, if the owner knows about such defect or could have discovered it by a reasonable inspection. Of course, as a responsible horse owner, you always check your hitch before you leave your barn, but this is another good reason to inspect it.

Some Miniature Horse owners may transport their horses in vehicles such as vans, station wagons, or pickup trucks with caps. While this eliminates the liability for trailer accidents, it is not necessarily better for either the owner of the vehicle or the horse itself. Almost all standard automobile policies exclude coverage for bodily injury or property damage expected or intended from the standpoint of the insured. This could mean that if you put your Miniature Horse in the back of your station wagon and it damages your vehicle, or somehow kicks or bites a passenger in your vehicle, there will—in all likelihood—be no insurance coverage provided for this type of occurrence. The insurance company will probably argue that such damage was expected or intended by you just by carrying an animal that is not normally transported in a passenger vehicle. Also, as previously mentioned, horses are not usually included in the general description of *"cargo"* or *"goods"* in an insurance policy except in the case of recognized usage to that effect, because horses are insurable in their own right. Additionally, the care, custody, or control exclusion in the policy would also exclude any coverage for any damage to the horse while it was owned by you or in your care, custody, or control.

While I have not specifically reviewed the numerous safety measures to be taken while trailering your Miniature Horse, it is clear that, in order to protect your investment and to treat the animal as humanely as possible, you should only transport your horse in a vehicle that is originally designed or modified to accommodate him. Because Miniature Horse trailers are very expensive, it is understandable that owners of these animals will want to find a more economical way to transport them. Aside from the animal's welfare, however, there are many concerns to be addressed with regard to the liability of taking such shortcuts which could result in situations both financially and emotionally costly for Miniature Horse owners. If you have been transporting your horse in a manner similar to those I've mentioned, you should review your automobile policy carefully and talk to your insurance agent to obtain the coverage that you need to transport your horse safely in a trailer. Regardless of how often you transport your horses, you should not neglect this aspect of your stable management.

Reprinted from Eastern Miniature, May 1992.

SECTION 5
The Money Side: Buying or Selling

Buying or Selling Your Miniature Horses
by Attorney Margaret Anderson-Murphy

At long last, you have found your next Miniature Horse Halter Champion, or broodmare, or simply the perfect backyard pet for your family. If your potential equine is the proverbial "gift horse," then you need not read any further. However, because the majority of us pay good money for our horses, it is important to consider the various aspects of the sale or purchase of a horse. Horsepeople have traditionally had a strong preference for dealing informally with one another, often closing the sale of a very expensive animal with a simple handshake and the exchange of cash for the animal's registration papers. In order to protect both parties, however, any sale of a horse should always be accompanied by a written sales agreement. While this need not be an elaborate document, it should contain all of the basic terms of the agreement, and any additional items which either party, or both parties want included. And, it should be signed by BOTH the buyer and the seller.

FROM THE SELLER'S POINT OF VIEW

If you are selling a horse, you should not make any promises that you cannot keep. This means that even if you are convinced that your horse is 100% sound and 100% sane, and the buyer's veterinarian confirms that the horse is, indeed, sound enough to pass a prepurchase examination, do not say so in the agreement. Any warranty that you make in writing to the buyer can easily come back to haunt you in the future. Six months down the road, the buyer may try to hold you responsible for the chronic lameness that has affected the horse since he purchased him from you.

Even if you make no affirmative representations about your horse, you can run up against future problems. Always include a disclaimer in your sales agreement stating that you are selling your horse *"as is"* or *"with all faults."* The reason for including these magic words is that the sale of horses is governed by what is known as *Article 2 of the Uniform Commercial Code*. Under the Code, unless the agreement contains a disclaimer, as the seller you implied warranty to the buyer that the horse you are selling is reasonably merchantable and suitable for the use and purpose to which he is normally put. In order to avoid any future claims against you if your horse does not turn out to be fit for the purpose for which you sold him (or any other purpose, for that matter), you should protect yourself by including the disclaimer clearly highlighted in the agreement.

Before you sell your horse, you should talk to the buyer and determine who is liable for the sales tax on the horse, if such a tax applies in your state. In many cases, it is the seller who pays the tax to the state or other local authorities and you should resolve this up front, so that when tax time rolls around there is no misunderstanding as to who owes the money for the horse.

Obviously you will have agreed upon a price with your buyer prior to making a sale. If your buyer has agreed to pay you in one lump sum, you would do well not to accept anything but a bank certified check or cash as payment for the horse. If your buyer has agreed to pay you in installments, then you should consider using a security agreement to protect your interest in the horse until the buyer has fully paid for him. In some cases, the seller may simply refuse to transfer the horse's registration papers until the contract has been paid in full. This type of arrangement will give you some leverage over the buyer if he or she wants to show or breed the animal. However, if you choose to hold on to the registration papers, you should notify the breed registry of the fact that you have taken a security interest on the horse by way of its certificate. This will help to prevent the issuance of a duplicate certificate by the registry, which may sometimes be attempted by an unscrupulous buyer. In order to fully protect yourself, I would not recommend this type of arrangement unless it is one that is fairly short term and involves a buyer whom you genuinely can trust. [*Editors note: In many instances involving the sale of expensive horses, the seller may require that the buyer take out a mortality insurance policy on the animal for the duration of the installment contract. This insures that, in the event of loss of the animal, both seller and buyer are protected.*]

In some instances, the buyer's purchase of a horse may be financed by you, the seller, or by a bank. In that case, you should (and the bank will) insist upon a written security agreement which contains, among other things, the names and addresses of the borrower and the lender, the nature of the sale that is giving rise to the security agreement, a description of the collateral (i.e., the horse, or any other collateral that may be supplied to secure the loan), and various other terms which protect you or the bank if the buyer fails to make his or her payments. In addition, no sales agreement or security agreement is complete as far as the seller is concerned unless it contains a provision giving the seller the right to recover attorney's fees and costs. In the event that a buyer fails to make all of his or her payments to you, you will then be entitled to collect the money that you spend to collect your money.

FROM A BUYER'S POINT OF VIEW

"Let the Buyer Beware" has never rung truer than when dealing with the purchase of a horse. As a buyer, you are taking a far greater risk in the transaction than is the seller. In order to protect yourself, you should be sure that the sales contract contains the exact name and address of the seller and the price of the horse, with all of the payment terms clearly spelled out, as well as a description of the horse which is identified by its breed registry number as well. Your sales contract should also contain some statement regarding the overall health of the horse, which may take the form of language such as "the horse has been examined by a veterinarian of the buyer's choice and, at the time of said examination, was found to be in good health and free of disease." Any statements regarding the soundness of the horse for breeding or other uses should be included if you are buying the horse for that specific purpose. As the buyer, you should be responsible for arranging and paying for a pre-purchase examination by a veterinarian of your choice. Some buyers like to use the seller's veterinarian because that individual is familiar with the horse and knows its past medical history. However, some people prefer to bring in their own veterinarian. This is reasonable, since this will probably be the veterinarian who will be seeing the horse in the future. He/she may bring a more objective approach to the examination, not having treated the horse in the past. If you are paying a significant amount of money for the horse and have big plans for its future, be sure to have the veterinarian do a complete and thorough workup. This should include x-rays, a pelvic exam and any other tests which the veterinarian feels are necessary to complete an accurate assessment of the horse's general health. Try to arrange for the veterinarian to examine the horse as close to the time of sale as possible.

In addition, your sales contract should state who will pay the sales tax on the horse, if such tax is applicable, whether you will pick up the horse from the seller's barn or whether the seller will deliver the horse to you, and the time and place of the sale. In order to be on the safe side, the seller should include a statement in the agreement warranting that he or she has clear title to the horse. In other words, he/she should be able to tell you that no other person has a lien against the horse for an unpaid board bill or other debt. Also, do not forget to discuss insurance with your seller and include a provision in your agreement specifying at what point the seller's insurance will stop covering the animal and yours will take effect.

Every sale of a horse has different circumstances which must be considered. For instance, if you are purchasing a broodmare who is in foal at the time of the sale, you should make arrangements to have the stallion service certificate delivered at the closing or have a copy of the stallion service contract available to you so that you are not surprised by any unpaid or unanticipated stud fees. Finally, do not forget to have the seller complete the transfer section on the horse's certificate of registration. Once the seller has delivered the certificate of registration to you, be sure to notify the breed registry of the horse's change of ownership as soon as possible.

THE OPTION OF LEASING

In some instances, it may be in the best interests of both the horse owner and the would-be buyer to lease the horse instead of selling it outright. As with a sales agreement, the lease should be written with all of the terms clearly spelled out and signed by both parties. At a minimum, the lease should contain the names and addresses of both the owner and the lessee, a description of the horse, the term of the lease (i.e., yearly or monthly), the lease fee and terms of its payment, and the various rights and responsibilities of both the owner and the lessee with regard to the horse. Up front, both parties should agree on who will be responsible for routine and emergency veterinary care and farrier services. In many instances, the lessee is responsible for the routine veterinary and blacksmith care, but in the event of a catastrophic illness or traumatic injury to the horse, the owner may step in and assist with the veterinary bills.

The owner should require that the lessee insure the horse under a mortality policy so that, in the event of the horse's death while it is in the care of the lessee, the owner will be able to recover the value of the horse. The parties should agree upon the stable where the horse is to be kept and, if it is to be transported for any reason, any specific precautions that should be taken with the horse should be spelled out in the lease. The lease should contain a provision that states that the lease agreement does not convey title to the lessee, and that the horse remains the property of the owner. There should also be a termination provision that allows one or both people to end the lease for whatever reasons the parties decide upon in advance.

Very importantly for the owner, the lessee should agree not to hold the owner liable for any accidents or injuries that involve the lessee while he/she is working around the horse. The lessee should also agree to indemnify the owner in the event that the owner is sued by another person who is hurt by the horse while he is being leased. The lease should provide for the collection of attorney's fees for the owner if the lessee fails to pay the lease fee and/or the board on the horse. In addition, if the lessee is willing, it is a good idea for the owner to obtain a first and last month's lease fee as security, which can then be refunded if the lessee terminates the lease and is fully paid up at the time. The details of any lease agreement should be worked out by both of the people involved and put in writing before the lease begins.

Buying a horse is a major investment. Once you have made the commitment to purchase or sell a horse, you should take all of the steps available to you to ensure that the transaction occurs without a problem. The same advice applies in a leasing situation, because you are involved in a long-term relationship with the owner or lessee, and things will go much more smoothly when you both have established written guidelines to define the terms of your agreement.

If you are considering the purchase of a very expensive horse, or even if you are involved in the sale or purchase of a moderately-priced horse, it is a good idea to consult an attorney before you sign anything. Any attorney will be willing to draft an agreement for you or review your agreement to make sure you have not left out any important terms that will come back to haunt you after the deal has been done. If you plan to use a security agreement, you should definitely consult an attorney to be sure that your document contains all of the necessary terms.

Ideally, after the sale and purchase of a horse, both people should walk away satisfied. Putting everything in writing will go a long way toward helping to accomplish that goal.

Reprinted from Eastern Miniature, July 1991.

The Hows & Whys of Syndication

The following two articles approach syndication from different angles. Attorney Margaret Anderson-Murphy gives the legal "nuts & bolts" of syndication as it has always been done. Long-time Miniature Horse owner/trainer Cheryl Lekstrom tells how this form of owning a stallion pertains to the Miniature Horse industry today.

Sharing The Wealth: Syndicating Your Stallion
by Margaret Anderson-Murphy

While the terms "syndicate" and the Thoroughbred stallion often go hand-in-hand, the concept of syndicating a successful stallion is not unique to race horses. The most common use of the term "syndicate" describes an arrangement in which mare owners go in together on the purchase of a stallion for breeding with their mares. This makes good sense, given the fact that a stallion can breed a large number of mares in a given season, and very few people own enough mares to fill a stallion's book. In order to spread the risk involved in purchasing an outstanding sire, the concept of selling undivided fractional interests in the stallion was developed.

With the values of some Miniature Horse stallions currently commanding six figures, owners may want to syndicate a successful stallion in order to lessen their own financial burdens, while retaining their rights to breed their mares to him.

(continued on page 95)

Syndication of Miniature Stallions
by Cheryl A. Lekstrom

The syndication of a stallion is not unfamiliar to the race horse or Arabian horse industry, but it is a new way of doing business for the American Miniature Horse industry. With Miniature show-quality stallions fetching $7,500 to $100,000, syndication provides an opportunity for the average person to acquire a portion of ownership of an otherwise untouchable commodity.

[At present] no established rules exist for setting up syndication of a Mini stallion. There is no standard contract, and at times the agreements between the syndicating parties are more like a closed booking contract, keeping the breeding rights to themselves, or a bit like a corporation that buys and sells different stallions in an attempt to make money on them. The agreements are simply defining the ownership of one or many different horses by many different people (shareholders) for many different reasons.

(continued on next page)

Miniature Stallions, con't

Today, we see syndication as a viable way for many people to pool their resources to acquire a nationally recognized bloodline that an individual person may not be able to afford. For people who already own a top quality stallion, but wish to diversify their bloodlines, it is a less expensive way to gain breeding access to other great blood. In the past, top quality Miniature Horse stallion owners rarely bred to outside mares because of mare quality, liability and disease issues, and if they did, it was at outrageous prices.

BASIC ORGANIZATION

Syndicates typically limit the number of owners (shareholders) and number of mares that the stallion may be bred to in a year. *NorthEast Syndicate* Administrator Chris Carbone commented that, *"It was originally thought that no breedings would be made to mares owned by anyone other than the shareholders in hopes that each shareholder would only breed their one best mare to the stallion."* However, there is provision for an individual shareholder to sell his breeding right to another mare owner. Each share is assigned a vote. It is interesting to note that a single share may be owned by a single person or in partnership.

The person who initiates the syndication typically becomes the Administrator or Manager of the syndication. This person is usually very involved in the breed so that all the advantages that the industry offers can be exploited. For example, the *NorthEast Syndicate's* yearling stallion, *Grosshill EK's Grand Illusion*, is entered in the American Miniature Horse Association (AMHA) Futurity and was also eligible for the Grosshill Farms/Hunt House Farms $10,000 Challenge.

The resulting benefit of a syndication is to make money on the breeding end of the business by being able to diversify your bloodline or sell the mare's resulting foal for top dollar. However, from the people I have spoken to, they seem more anxious to get their syndicated stallion's blood into their barn and keep it there.

Insurance companies will insure the shares of the syndicate for the shareholder, which is important since they estimate that the shares can be worth 3 or 4 times what they originally paid for them. *"It is extremely important that, if you do find a horse that you want to syndicate, you are 90% sure in your mind that it is a quality horse by being a winner and good sire. Do not syndicate mediocre stallions because, in the long run, you will have problems meeting the standards for him. Know what your probabilities are. If you really want to gamble on a young horse, know that you are,"* cautioned one administrator.

A syndication is only as good as the manager of it and his/her ability to promote and stand the stallion, or find someone who will. If you are able to breed your mare to your syndicated stallion year after year and get live foals, then you have probably already realized a return on your investment.

Syndication fees are usually less or equal to a stud fee in the long run. The initial investment can be from $2,000.00 to $8,500.00 to own a piece of a prized stallion. Maintenance costs can be as little as $86.00 a year to hundreds of dollars per year per share.

To get out of a syndication, you may either sell your share (*watch out, sometimes second-hand shares carry no vote or have other limitations*) or forfeit. If enough people forfeit their shares, the horse reverts back to the original owner or the initiator of the syndicate.

To invest in a yearling or unproven colt is to wait longer for your return on investment. In breeding horses there are no guarantees, so you need to assess how much risk you are willing to assume and at what price. One would hope that the younger the horse, the more risk, and the lower the price. You need to carefully consider the stallion. He may be a National winner this year, but who will win next year?

MINIATURE HORSE SYNDICATION TODAY

I have been able to locate only six Miniature Horse syndicates to date: the very first one was founded in 1988 for the purpose of sharing the promotional expenses and breeding rights for a group of people who didn't have a national caliber stallion for their breeding purposes.

The NorthEast Syndicate was founded in 1994. In *The NorthEast Syndicate* agreement, the syndicate is defined as, " *...an association of persons who combine to carry out the financial enterprise of underwriting the showing, breeding, and sales of Miniature Horses for profit."*

The NorthEast Syndicate was put together to go out and buy a specific stallion, *Grosshill EK's Grand Illusion*. To accomplish this, each shareholder put enough money into the pot to buy their share of the horse, plus additional monies to pay for feeding, care, insurance, showing, administrative fees and maintenance of the horse. The shareholder may share in a portion of the proceeds of the prize money, premiums, gifts, awards, futurity winnings, insurance benefits, profit from sale of the horse, etc. for a designated amount of time. The shareholder may also share in any losses: death of the horse, medical, legal, arbitration, and accounting expenses.

The NorthEast Syndicate has been written with provisions for selling the horse at a profit and acquiring other stallions as the association sees fit. The members are assessed additional fees as the escrow account is depleted. Telephone conference calls are made to discuss any significant expenses or promotional opportunities.

One shareholder in *The NorthEast Syndicate* was thrilled to be able to attend the National AMHA show in Ohio her first year to cheer on her stallion from box seats. She saw this syndication as a chance to own and breed to a national caliber horse that she would not be able to afford to show or commit to train and promote on her own. She said that she would not have been able to get one of her own horses qualified and presented without sending it to a professional handler. So in a way, when you buy into a syndication, you also get all the years of experience and the reputation of the farm that commits to board and show the horse.

The Buck Echo Syndicate, also founded in 1994 by Little King Farm of Madison, IN was a situation where the breeder kept half the ownership of the horse and syndicated the other half to four different investors. *Little King's Buck Echo* made his owners very happy that year by taking home the 1994 National Grand Champion Senior Stallion title, as well as being the proven sire of the 1994 National Champion Weanling Filly. He is the smallest National Grand Champion Senior Stallion in history. For one of the shareholders, the most important part of their decision to enter into a syndication was that, *"the stallion be mature, with a nationally-recognized bloodline with consistent big winnings from that bloodline by a syndicate manager who has demonstrated lots of success in the Miniature Horse business."* These investors are in *The Buck Echo Syndicate* for the life of the horse and already feel it is the best money they ever spent in their four years of Miniature Horse investing.

A syndication contract may be written to include many different variables. *The Buck Echo Syndicate* does not charge its shareholders for board or a management fee since the horse is still at home. Syndication was a good way for the breeder to get enough money to properly promote the *Buck Echo* bloodline without giving him up. And it was a big win for the people lucky enough to become part of his syndication.

With race horse syndication, a stallion may breed hundreds of mares per year using Artificial Insemination (A.I.) techniques. The American Miniature Horse Association does not recognize A.I., so the number of mares a mature stallion can successfully breed to is limited. Miniature Horse mares are sent to the stallion and are kept there until they are confirmed in foal or may even be foaled out at the stallion's farm. Here again, the syndicate manager must be savvy enough to have nominated the stallion for the AMHA futurity so that the offspring will be valuable and a return on investment may be acknowledged.

To commit to keep, condition, show and promote a syndicated stallion is demanding and could become a problem if no one wants to do that part of it. Who will show the horse and at what shows may be voted on by the shareholders. *The NorthEast Syndicate* only shows their horse at prestigious shows pointed by the AMHA toward National titles. *"The intention is that the horse will be shown only against other top horses in the breed,"* according to that syndicate's administrator. The association agreed that their horse will not be shown at local small shows or exhibitions.

With over 35 years' experience in the Arabian Horse business, Ray Zoercher and Gary McMorrow decided to syndicate a gorgeous palomino stallion, *Little Trigger*, and his palomino son, *Fairy Tail's Prince*, as a favor to their good friends and clients. The syndicates have boosted the camaraderie of the five shareholders and the marketability of the horses.

These two syndications are very formal and were started by offering a total of 24 shares on each horse. The units were sold in groups of four shares. Each share equals one breeding per year with a live foal guarantee for *Little Trigger* who stands at Freedom Hill Farm. A half-breeding is available for *Fairy Tail's Prince* because he is on the show circuit.

The syndicate contracts are complete and thorough with an addendum that is filed with AMHA as to the list of shareholder owners. The horses are registered with AMHA in the name of their syndicates, with the agents also named.

GOOD INVESTMENTS

Miniature Horses are a good investment. When you put together the initial cost of the horse, stabling, and care requirements, you are making a significant investment. Even the insurance industry knows that you are not bringing home a pet. The many different benefits may be monetary, social and therapeutic.

The opportunity to join a syndication is limited. The last four syndicates to be formed were by private invitation to other Miniature Horse owners. However, as the syndicates either dissolve or mature, their syndication may be advertised to the public by the splitting or adding of shares. There is no doubt in my mind that syndications will become more popular as the base of Miniature Horse enthusiasts expands.

Sharing The Wealth, con't

Before you decide to syndicate your stallion, you should consider a few basic issues. Some of those issues include:

1) whether you are willing to share your horse;
2) whether you can sell interests in your horse;
3) whether you are prepared to handle administrative matters; and
4) whether you want to limit the number of mares that are bred to your horse.

Once you have decided to syndicate, you should reduce the syndicate agreement to writing. While the exact nature of the syndicate agreement may vary from stallion to stallion, a basic agreement should include a division of the ownership of the horse and subsequent assignment of the fractional interests to the various owners. The agreement should also identify a syndicate manager who will supervise the care and breeding of the stallion and the agreement should spell out his or her duties clearly, as well. In choosing a syndicate manager, you should carefully examine the manager's financial condition and whether he or she can bring mares to your stallion. In order to induce an individual to act as a syndicate manager, your syndicate agreement should include language limiting the liability of the syndicate manager for any injury, disease, or death which may occur to any horse during the performance of the syndicate manager's duties. Finally, the agreement should have provisions which address liability insurance to protect the members of the syndicate from any liability caused by a stallion, and should address the payment of expenses by the syndicate manager or other authorized person.

SYNDICATE MEMBERS' OPTIONS

The owner of each fractional interest in a stallion holds an annual right to breed, known as a *"nomination"* or a *"season."* Usually, the agreement will provide that the owner of a season will be entitled to nominate one mare to be bred to the stallion during each breeding season. The total number of nominations or seasons make up the stallion's *"book"* of mares. If it becomes necessary to reduce or expand the stallion's normal book, the syndicate agreement should provide for a method of determining how the members will resolve the change in the stallion's number of breedings per season. Needless to say, in order to protect the stallion, the syndicate agreement should define the health requirements of the mares which are to be bred to him.

In addition to the right of each syndicate member to breed one or more mares to the stallion, the syndicate agreement should provide for other rights and obligations of the members, including the calling of a syndicate meeting to discuss business matters relating to the syndicate. The members usually also agree to pay a pro-rata share of the expenses involved in the agreement, such as veterinary bills, farrier costs, accounting and legal fees, and other expenses. In the event that a member decides to sell his or her fractional interests, the agreement should provide for a right of first refusal to any other member who may wish to purchase another member's fractional interest before it is offered to the general public.

While a syndicate agreement (if done right) can both benefit and protect its members, it is not without disadvantages. Sometimes the state of the economy makes syndicate shares difficult to sell. In addition, as with any undertaking, the greater the number of people involved with the

TYPES OF SYNDICATION

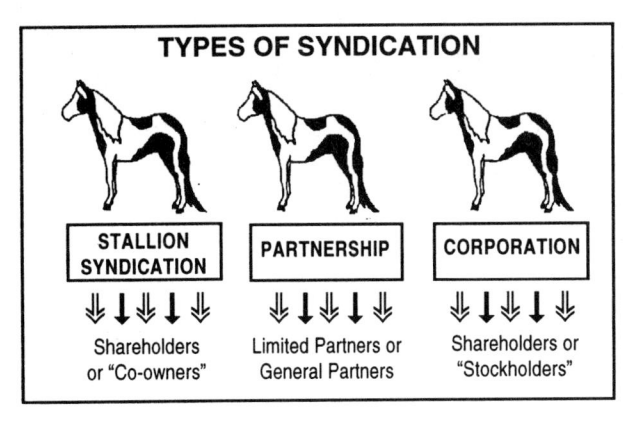

STALLION SYNDICATION — Shareholders or "Co-owners"

PARTNERSHIP — Limited Partners or General Partners

CORPORATION — Shareholders or "Stockholders"

stallion, the more complicated and less flexible the management of the stallion becomes.

Syndicate agreement is not the only method by which to stand a stallion. Sole proprietorships, partnerships, and corporations can be crafted to serve the same purpose as a typical syndicate agreement, as well as incorporating the various advantages offered by each of these alternative business forms. In order to determine which form would best serve your needs, you should consult an attorney.

STALLION SEASONS

Every time the owner of a stallion sells a season, the sale should be documented by means of a "stallion service contract." Again, these documents vary according to the needs of the people involved, but generally, there are three basic categories of seasons. The one most commonly used is the "**live foal**" season. In this case, the stallion owner bears the risk that the mare will not conceive as a result of being bred to the stallion. Although the mare is typically bred in the spring, the mare's owner does not pay the stud fee to the stallion owner until the fall. If the mare produces a live foal which is able to stand alone and nurse, the stallion owner keeps the stud fee. But, if the mare does not conceive, aborts the fetus, or the foal is never, in fact, able to stand and nurse, then the stud fee is returned to the mare owner. In order for the mare owner to receive his or her money back, however, it is usually necessary for him or her to produce a veterinarian's certificate stating that the foal, for whatever reason, did not live.

The second type of season is the "**no guaranty**" season. As the name implies, the season is sold to the mare owner without any guarantee that the mare will produce a foal from the breeding. Given the fact that the mare owner has to bear a larger risk, this type of season is substantially less expensive than a live foal season. At the time the stallion service contract is entered into, the mare owner normally pays a non-refundable fee. The horse insurance industry has developed live foal insurance that can help to decrease the risks associated with the purchase of a no guaranty season. If you auction off your stallion's seasons, this is usually the preferred method of doing so, since it allows the transaction to be final at the auction itself.

The third type of season is a combination of a **"live foal and a no guaranty"** season. The mare owner usually agrees to pay a nonrefundable fee upon the execution of the stallion service contract and agrees to pay an additional amount later if the mare produces a live foal. This is probably the least commonly used type of season, given its nature.

As with any contract, a stallion service contract should contain basic information regarding names and addresses of the buyer and seller, as well as the amount of the stud fee, the type of season that is being sold (live foal or no guaranty), and various representations regarding the health of the horses involved.

In the final analysis, once the agreement is put in writing to the satisfaction of everyone concerned, it all comes down to what occurs in the breeding shed. Once the potential legal problems have been addressed, care should be taken to avoid injury and disease to the stallion. Given their size, Minis will probably not present as much of a problem as full-sized horses, but because your stallion represents your investment, you should take all precautions to protect him. As a stallion owner, you will, of course, want to examine all mares who are brought to your stallion to ensure that they are healthy and not likely to hurt the stallion during the breeding.

Syndicating a valuable stallion has sound economic and practical advantages. In order to avoid as many problems as possible, make sure to get all of the terms in your agreement clearly defined in writing before the breeding season begins, so that you do not lose valuable opportunities to breed your stallion due to a problem with the paperwork.

Reprinted from Eastern Miniature, September 1991.

Top-notch Pictures Sell Horses!
Preparing For the Photographer
by Toni M. Leland

We have all tried to take pictures of our own horses, present company included. Rolls of film, hours of exertion (especially for action shots!) and the incredible disappointment as you look at them in the car outside the Fast Foto shop brings one to the conclusion that it isn't all that easy! Next step—call a "Pro."

We interviewed several top equine photographers from around the country in order to compile the information you need to make the most of your investment with a "Pro." These "artists" are well-known and photograph many breeds, including some who do Miniature Horses. The final photo is, in fact, up to you—knowing what to expect and providing your cooperation are essential to the success of the person behind the camera.

HOW FAR AHEAD SHOULD YOU PLAN?

Without exception, the photographers we interviewed agreed that a large number of their jobs were "RUSH." Being flexible is part of a photographer's job, but if you know you'll want shots of your stallion for spring, or baby pictures for marketing your foals, you should contact the photographer early and have him/her make a tentative date that you can firm up as the time approaches. This way, you won't wait until the last minute and be disappointed because he/she is booked and can't make it when you are ready.

WHAT DO YOU NEED TO DO BEFORE THE PHOTOGRAPHER ARRIVES?

Allow plenty of time for the shoot. Don't try to sandwich the photographer's visit in between other appointments, such as showing horses for sale or the veterinarian's visit. If you are having only one horse photographed, you can figure the actual time (once everything is ready) to be 1 to 1½ hours of camera time. Allow a couple of extra hours for preliminary work and inspection and time used between setups. For more than one horse, figure a half-day or more, depending on the number of animals being photographed. Take into consideration capricious weather. The fog may take an extra hour to lift, or the sun may disappear for awhile. Certain times of day are best for outdoor photography and your photographer can tell you what he/she prefers. Horses may be uncooperative and extend the amount of time needed to get good shots. Patience is the key word on this day and your photographer shouldn't have to compete with other events.

Your horse or horses should be ready—show ready: bathed, clipped, brushed and feet prepared. DON'T clip your horses the day of or the day before the picture session. A week before the date is a good rule of thumb— this allows the clipper marks to grow out and smooth over. The camera will see things that your naked eye cannot. Remember, the photographs will most likely be used for promotion of your horses and the animal must look the best it can. Last minute touch-ups are okay, but don't ask the photographer to wait while you clip or dry a horse.

The halters you will use should be spotless, just as they would for a show. And, if your horses wear heavy barn halters all the time, be sure to take them off early and brush the marks away before putting on a fine show halter that sits in a different spot on the horse's nose. The camera WILL pick up the indentation in the hair. Use a good lead that matches or goes with the halter—no ropes!

Have yourself or your handler dressed appropriately. Show clothes aren't necessary unless that's the look you're aiming for, but something other than barn grubbies, please! Sometimes that "perfect" picture will include an arm or part of the handler and cropping things out of pictures has its limits.

Have an idea what pictures you have in mind. Do you have a favorite spot on the farm? Are you looking for an artistic shot with black background or special effects? Head shots or body shots? Or both? Posed or at liberty? Think about the purpose of your pictures. What areas are you concentrating on—sales of stock, breeding, show horses?

Have the horse(s) "tuned up" before your photographer arrives. A little exercise to wake him up and make him interested in what is going on can help ensure an alert look when the shutter starts snapping. Our contact photographers who do Minis agreed that the laid back attitude of the Miniature Horse makes it challenging to get that special look. If at all possible, have the horses' regular handler present at the shooting session. An uncertain or nervous atmosphere will only upset the horses and make them uncooperative.

WHAT WILL YOU NEED TO HAVE ON HAND?

If you are the regular handler, be sure to have an extra person available to hold things, get the horse's attention, and do anything else that might be needed. Have a bucket or bag to carry items to the various spots chosen for pictures. Fly spray, a towel, grooming spray, an extra halter (in case one breaks), and a brush for touch-ups—good to have them handy rather than run back to the barn. Time is important here, since animals tend to lose interest in what's going on if they stand around too long. If your photographer is coming from a distance, it's a good idea to have the usual props available, since most photographers don't carry things other than their equipment when flying. Mirrors, plastic bags, a balloon—whatever you think might get a good response—assemble these beforehand. When you initially make a date with the photographer, ask if there is anything special he/she likes to use as attention-getters.

WHAT SHOULD YOU EXPECT ONCE YOUR PHOTOGRAPHER ARRIVES?

Most photographers will want to "case the joint" to see where potential sites are, take light readings, and check for shadow factors. Use this time for your final touch-ups and to get your thoughts together.

Be prepared to take direction from the photographer once the shoot begins. As a professional, he/she knows when to shoot, what the overall pictures will be like, and what can be controlled on the final film. Your suggestions and comments are most welcome before the session begins, but are very distracting once photographers get into what they are doing. Concentrate on giving him/her what is needed and, above all, resist the temptation to tell him when you think he should press the shutter button! The less outside contributions from those in attendance, the better.

Try to be as relaxed as possible about the whole thing, because any tension on your part will be transmitted to the horse, who may then become difficult. Don't worry about whether the pictures will turn out—most professional photographers will redo the shoot if you really don't like any of your proofs. Expect your photographer to be professional, have plenty of film, and all the necessary equipment he/she might need for various settings and light situations.

HOW SOON SHOULD YOU EXPECT PROOFS AND PRINTS?

All our photographers said that 1½ to 2 weeks was standard for getting proofs to the client. Additional charges are made for RUSH jobs, since the photographer has to pay rush charges to the processing lab. Once you've chosen your proofs and sent in your order, the time for turn-around is 3-4 weeks for these custom prints. Retouching or special effects will add as much as a week to ten days to that time. And, obviously, during the show season, demand is high for photographs and the times stated could be delayed somewhat.

HOW MUCH WILL THIS COST YOU?

Clearly, each photographer has their own individual pricing structure, but these all fall within general guidelines. Standard payment policies are: full payment for farm call in advance or on the day of the shoot, and full payment with the order for prints and special charges.

Farm calls range from $100 per day plus expenses to $300 per day plus expenses. On combined farm calls in an area, the travel expenses are usually divided equally. Most photographers charge a film and processing fee of $25-35 per roll with an average of 1-2 rolls of film taken per horse.

Rush charges are usually about double the cost of the print. Express shipping charges are billed at cost on rush jobs. Retouching (airbrushing) can run from $11 to $50 per print, depending on the result required and the artist or lab used.

Quantity discounts can save you as much as 20%, and allows you some flexibility, in that you are not caught with one photo and three ads to do! Seriously consider getting together with other farms in the area so that the cost of your farm call can be reduced. Photographers are very agreeable to this, as it also makes better use of their time.

A WORD ABOUT COPYRIGHTS

Photographers all over the country feel very strongly about abuse of copyright.
"When it's printed, it's copyrighted."

Just as an author, a painter, or a composer "owns" the creation he has conceived, a photographer's pictures are an embodiment of his art, and this is his livelihood.

While equine photography is used almost exclusively for promotion and advertising, as opposed to pictures for pleasure, the owner of the subject never owns the photograph. The print you purchase is usually sold with the condition that it will be reproduced only for your personal advertising and only with a signature or photographer's credit given on the ad. Some prints will be stamped "One-time exclusive use with permission" which means that technically, they may only be used one time. The commercial photographer in the business world usually sells exclusive rights and then receives a royalty each time the picture is reproduced in any form. Obviously, this would be over-kill in the equine industry.

Traditionally, show photos are done up on "contact sheets" where every frame on the strip of film is printed at its original size (1" x 1") on a large sheet of print paper. To really see these proofs, one needs a magnifying glass. For the private client, prints are usually made up and these proofs are stamped "Not for Reproduction" and copyrighted, but not signed. A large, usable proof is a courtesy extended by the photographer. To protect his or her picture, the photographer must mark the proof in a manner to make it unusable—sometimes to the detriment of the clarity of the subject. One of our contacts makes up show prints (proofs) of the best shots, signs them, and marks the back with copyright and ordering information. They are mailed to the exhibitor with an invoice and the request for return, if not purchased. This is truly the Honor System and this particular photographer stated that, for the most part, the prints were usually paid for.

Any reputable printer, advertising agency, film developer, or copy shop will usually refuse to duplicate a proof or signed photograph. If, in the course of a design layout, the signature is cropped out, then credit must be given directly underneath the photograph on the ad layout. Almost without exception, magazine publishers will not print photographs that are obviously proofs, unless the photographer has given written permission. To do so is to invite litigation. To use proofs for advertising, even in the local club newsletter, is—quite simply put—stealing.

Reprinted from Eastern Miniature, November 1991.

SECTION 6
Training and Showing Miniature Horses

Basics of Driving
by Ted Garman

In most driving classes at Miniature Horse shows, one or more of the horses will simply be pulling the cart around the show ring, rather than being driven. A vast difference exists between the two and this is what determines whether the horse and driver are in the blue and red ribbons or out the gate. The following includes a few, important points to consider when showing a driving horse.

The author demonstrates an example of very good collection.

Just as a person should take lessons in golf or tennis to be a competitive player, one should attend several driving clinics and consider having a professional train the horse. It is very difficult to beat years of experience and special talent in any game.

A horse that is well-trained and properly driven will give the impression that it is enjoying the drive. A well-conditioned horse will go at ease, showing no tell-tale signs of fatigue often seen at shows. The horse will appear and, in fact, be bolder, stronger, and appear to cover the ground ever so lightly. These are some things that either make the horse stand out from the rest or merely blend in and go unnoticed.

SELECTING A DRIVING HORSE

One should start with *The American Miniature Horse Standard of Perfection* adopted by the American Miniature Horse Association (AMHA). (see Appendix) [Ed.note: *Standard of Perfection* for American Miniature Horse Registry is also located in Appendix.] In addition to this reference, the following points deserve special note.

Feet: The feet should be free of faults. Hooves that are abnormally shaped, contracted heels, or other peculiarities which may interfere with the horse's stride and endurance should be avoided.

Pasterns: The pastern should slope about 45 degrees and should be on the same angle as the hoof and shoulder. Avoid springy pasterns and pasterns that slope too little or too much. A springy pastern is an indication of weakness and will not hold up under the stress of prolonged use. Pasterns that are too steeply sloped cause the horse to have a short, choppy stride, hindering its endurance and limiting its ability to cover ground.

Legs: Straight legs are a must. After you have seen a front, rear and side view to make sure the legs are straight, have someone lead the horse straight away from you. Observe carefully to make sure that there is no winging, dishing or other deviation from a straight line movement of each leg. Many times, crooked legs will show up in the horse's movement. After viewing movement from the rear at the walk and trot, view the horse from the side at both gaits. When walking, the rear hoof should step near or in the track of the front hoof on the same side. This should be true at a trot as well. The horse's legs should be in proportion to the rest of the body. Short legs are definitely a disadvantage in a driving horse.

Body: Bodies that are too long, too short or too large relative to the legs are hardships to driving. A barrel (chest and rib cage) adequate to maintain good breathing is a necessity. A fairly wide chest with shoulders at a 45 degree angle complement a good driving horse. Shoulders that are steeper cause the horse's stride to be too choppy and short; such a horse cannot go for very long, nor can it achieve much speed.

Head & Neck: The head and neck serve important functions to balance the rest of the animal. The neck, first of all, should be flexible. It should easily flex from left to right; a flexible neck is necessary to negotiate turns and to react quickly. The head balances the rest of the body. If it is thick and does not have a clear throatlatch, flexion is restricted and so is balance.

A thick neck restricting flexion hinders collection. To understand collection, which is most important in driving, try to think of how a rider achieves collection. The horse's head is raised, flexing at the poll, taking on a swan-like silhouette (especially if the horse has a flexible, well-proportioned neck). With the head being raised and the neck and poll flexed, the center of gravity of the horse is shifted to the rear. This backward shifting of the center of gravity causes the horse to drive off the hind legs. Relative to its body weight, a horse's head is heavier than other animals' heads. When the head is held low and the nose pointing out, the horse has to try to pull more weight with its front legs. This action puts more stress on the front legs. The hind legs are built for propulsion of the horse. In collection, the heavy work is given to the hind legs, allowing the front legs to achieve more action.

The head should be carried with the forehead almost perpendicular to the ground. The chin should not be tucked in, nor should the nose be pointed out. Head carriage will vary among horses due to their overall conformation. A longer, thinner neck can and should be held higher than a shorter, thicker neck. The higher a short neck is carried, the more the nose will stick out, tending to cause the horse to amble. Furthermore, breathing and balance will be restricted.

HARNESS PARTS THAT NEED SPECIAL ATTENTION IN DRIVING

A good profile and overall striking topline look (from the head carriage all the way back to the croup) is impressive to a judge or any other observer. To achieve this, several parts of the harness are involved. Starting from the mouth of the horse and going down the center of the top line, the harness parts involved are as follows:

Overcheck—this connects the bit through the bridle to the saddle. Shortening the overcheck raises the head. Lengthening it lowers the head. Once the head is raised to the desired height, the driver uses the reins to further set the head by pulling the nose back. Overcheck bits are not used on Miniature Horses. On these small horses, a single bit is sufficient.

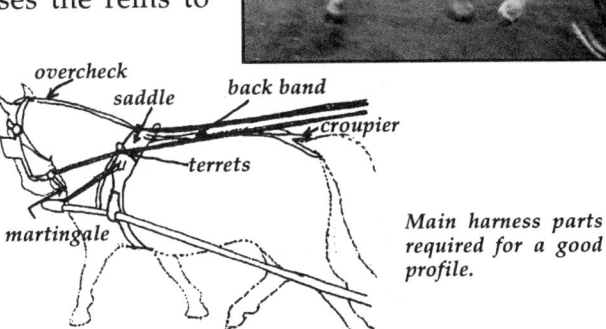

Main harness parts required for a good profile.

Training & Showing Miniature Horses

Saddle—the saddle serves as a central anchor point. All other parts of the harness are attached or pass through the saddle. It is important not to over-tighten the saddle, nor have it too loose which causes loss of control. If it is too tight, it restricts breathing and causes discomfort which can cause the horse to look sour or mean. When it is too loose, the cart will jerk on starts and flop around. Good judgement should be used in tightening the saddle; it must be snug, but not binding.

Croupier—the back strap connects the croupier to the saddle. The bit, overcheck, saddle, back strap and croupier are connected in one line from head to tail. To be functional, these parts should not be loose. After all are adjusted, have someone drive the horse and look at its topline, starting with the head carriage. If a higher head carriage is needed, the overcheck or the back strap may be adjusted. If the saddle is in the proper position, the overcheck may be tightened. To lower the head, loosen the overcheck. Trial and adjustment is required to achieve the best topline suited to the horse's conformation. The horse's head should not be checked way up, at first. This will cause the horse discomfort and it will show displeasure by rearing or shaking the head. It is preferable to gradually raise the head with the overcheck over a period of weeks in training.

HARNESSING AND HITCHING TO THE CART

The horse should be hitched when the handler is satisfied that the horse is ready. Establishing a routine of hitching and following it each time will develop more trust and confidence on the part of the horse. A good routine to use when working alone is:

1. At the area where the horse is to be hitched, place all needed equipment within arm's reach.
2. Lead the haltered horse to the spot and securely tie it there.
3. Proceed with the harness saddle, loosely tightened, then the croupier, and the breast collar with the traces. Then pull the martingales through the breast collar.
4. Hitch the horse to cart, making all the necessary adjustments. Check the belly band for proper adjustment.
5. Remove the halter and put the bridle on, threading the reins through the martingale and then through the rein turrets. The

handler should be sure to maintain control of the horse at all times and should never use the bit or bridle to tie the horse. A good rule is to hitch in an area where the horse cannot escape if it does get away from you.

GROUND DRIVING

Ground driving is a good way of reviewing the basic commands and to warm up the horse for conditioning and training. In addition, ground driving is a good way to establish communication and control of the horse. This is effective in getting the playfulness or "wire edge" off before hooking the horse to the cart. Even before ground driving, longeing or putting the horse on a walker will work off the tendency to play or jump around.

Once the harness is properly fitted, adjusted and all loose ends taken care of, ground driving can begin. During ground driving, basic training should be reviewed for the benefit of the horse. When the command to *"walk"* is given, the handler should be acutely aware of the mouth. Great care should be taken not to "get in" the horse's mouth (too heavy a hand-pressure on the bit), as this will cause resistance. The horse may shake its head, open its mouth, lay back its ears or display other gestures of displeasure. These signs will be penalized in the show ring, especially in a pleasure driving class.

The author shows ground driving techniques

When the horse moves out, the handler should go with it while maintaining even pressure on the bit. When the horse is asked to *"trot,"* the handler must increase speed to match the horse, keeping the same even pressure on the bit.

After the command *"whoa"* is given and the horse comes to a complete stop, he should stand still, preferably square. The horse should respond to the command to "back." This completes the more important commands. If the horse does not comply during any of the review, repetition of some commands may be necessary. Five minutes or so of ground driving will probably be enough.

Ground driving should include circles in both directions, figure eights, and going around obstacles. This will put both the horse's mind and that of the handler on the task at hand.

DRIVING

In pleasure driving, according to the *Official Rule Book of the AMHA*, the horse is to be judged 60 percent on performance, manners and way of going; 30 percent on the condition, fit and appropriateness of harness and vehicle; and 10 percent on neatness, appropriateness of attire, and overall impression. This should be kept in mind when training for and competing in the show ring. The following points will be most helpful.

When a horse is being ridden, the rider's aids include contact with the mouth through the hands and bit, contact with the body by using positioning and leg pressure, the whip, and the voice. Body contact and leg pressure is lost in driving and the other aids must compensate for this loss. Many drivers attempt to drive their horses without the aid of a whip. They are placing an unnecessary handicap upon themselves. The whip serves as an extension of the hand and is quite valuable in achieving and maintaining collection in the driving horse. Just as a rider will urge a horse forward with the legs, a driver signals the horse with a touch of the whip. While asking for collection with the whip, the driver should signal through the reins as well. For a trained horse, tightening ever so slightly on the reins and a touch of the whip is the signal for collection. Tightening the reins brings the horse's nose in, shifting the center of gravity toward the rear legs. The horse must then drive off the hind legs. When the horse's head is raised and the nose is reined in to about perpendicular, some weight is shifted from the front legs. A horse is said to be going on the forehand when much of the propulsion is with the front legs. The driving horse should "drive" off its hind legs. These legs have the muscles for this purpose. The horse will look better, have a much better topline, and will be able to travel a longer distance before tiring.

The horse and driver should enter the gate giving an impressive look. The horse should be collected and enter at the collected trot. The driver should sit erect at all times, be dressed appropriately, and present an overall appearance that the event is pleasurable.

The horse will give a better appearance if it is in good condition. A horse in poor condition will tire easily and look sour, causing it to be placed lower in the class. It is unfair to the horse to bring it to a show in poor condition. Conditioning takes several months of preparation, so start your program well in advance of show season.

GAITS

Once in the ring, the important characteristics of the gaits are described as follows:

Walk—The walk should be a steady, ground-covering gait with the hind foot stepping in or near the track left by the front foot. The walk should be brisk, but not deteriorate into an amble.

Collected Trot—The collected trot is steady and well-cadanced. The horse should look like it could keep up this gait all day. The gait should cover ground and not degenerate into a sloppy-appearing, loose gait. Reins should maintain contact at all times, without sagging, but at the same time, not exerting too much pressure (*"getting in the horse's mouth"*).

Working Trot—The working trot should be brisk, snappy, animated and showy. The horse should be driven off the hocks, not bounding on the forehand. Long strides should be exhibited and will make the horse appear to float off the ground at the point when all four feet are actually off the ground. Excessive speed will be penalized in the pleasure driving class.

The attitude of the horse and driver should be one of pleasure. The horse should not present a strained appearance and, likewise, the driver should look like he's having a good time.

A little final advice. When you don't know, ask a pro. A true professional trainer and exhibitor likes to compete with the best. He or she will readily answer your questions and give advice or instructions. Attend driving clinics; if there aren't any in your area, call around and get one organized. What you learn may very well put you in the Blue. Happy Driving!

Reprinted from Eastern Miniature, May 1991.

Sport Horse In Miniature
by Cheryl A. Lekstrom

Miniature Horses with many talents are becoming the lunch-time entertainment at large breed horse shows and the draw at equine expositions around the country. Hunting, jumping, and driving classes are included in all American Miniature Horse Association (AMHA) recognized shows* and are real crowd pleasers. The classes are divided between novice, youth, amateur and professional participants to give every level of exhibitor and horse a chance to win. The colorful courses are set up to be pleasing to the spectators as well as challenging to the horses.

This Miniature Horse exhibits the proper form as he takes a jump on the hunt course.

Great enthusiasm is generated by watching a Miniature take jumps with style, grace and precision. All of my horses tend to be good jumpers, teaching themselves by leaping over their stall doorjambs. It's only a matter of them learning to pace themselves on the course, judge different heights and grow accustom to different looking jumps. They seem to relish the challenge, and once they have learned that I am not going to ask them to do anything that might injure them, they enjoy jumping over flower boxes, cross poles, lattice, simulated stone walls, water, and coops.

You can develop your Miniature into a fairly good hunter/jumper or driving horse in three months. However, years are spent honing a horse to perfection in both of these disciplines. You will need to find a horse at least three years old that you enjoy working with and one that shows talent and potential in these areas. You will need to handle him at least thirty minutes daily, if not several times a day.

HUNTER VERSUS JUMPER

In a *Hunter* class the horse is judged on style, manners and way of going with preference given to those horses covering the course with free flowing strides. The horse should jump the fences in the middle, not too high, not too low, at a nice even pace (trot or canter), taking off with room to spare, tucking the legs up evenly, having a nice roll to the back and landing evenly and controlled. The exhibitor may not go over the jump or carry a whip. You will be eliminated if your horse refuses three times, if you go off course, cross your own path, or if you or your horse fall.

In a *Jumper* class, it doesn't matter how the horse goes over the jump, so long as he clears it. Horses are judged on accumulated faults: knockdowns, refusals, crossing your own path, going off course, a fall of the horse and/or exhibitor, with elimination for three refusals. The jumps are raised in a process of elimination. The exhibitor may carry a whip, wear sneakers and go over the jumps with the horse. This is the class where we saw a jumper clear 44 inches at the National Show in 1991.

You will observe many styles in the jump class: *the leapfrog*, the young horse who consistently jumps the rail with lots of room to spare; *the popper*, who has an even cadence until he reaches the jump, pauses, then pops over and resumes his gait; *the twister*, who corks his body over the highest of jumps; *the sidewinder*, who jumps everything off-center, and *the crash & burn*, "I'm going through it for no particular reason and without warning." I love to watch this class because I know that with a lot more practice and a little guidance, most of these horses are going to make beautiful hunters some day.

GETTING STARTED

Always warm your horse up with a minimum ten minutes of alternate walking and trotting before asking him to take even the lowest jump. Build height slowly over days and weeks, four to six inches a week. Never sacrifice the jumping form of your horse for height. It is better to have a horse jump in proper form than to ask him to jump too high and discourage him from jumping altogether by rapping his feet on the rails.

To initially teach your horse to jump, lay a pole on the ground and encourage him to go over it as in cavaletti training. Raise the pole four inches and ask him to go over it at a trot. At this point, I use a cross rail to teach the horse where the middle of the jump is—it will be the lowest, easiest point to jump in the middle. I will raise this jump to a foot or more before making it a solid rail with the center marked by paint or tape. Always use a ground rail in front of the jump to give the horse a visual reference of the jump. And always "fill in" the jump with rails as you go higher so that the entire jump to the top rail has a visual reference. Don't leave a lot of air between the top and bottom rails as the horse may try to go through the jump rather than over it.

Only jump things that can fall free should the horse bang a leg or foot on it. Never jump sharp objects—including poorly manufactured jump cups with sharp edges. If your horse injures himself when you ask him to jump something that won't fall free, he may never trust you enough to jump anything again. PVC poles wrapped with colored tape to give the horse a sense of depth make the best, safest jumps. Always top off a flower box jump, coop, or lattice with a PVC pipe to knock down before he gets into trouble in the flowers or lattice. Lay rags over the poles to change their appearance. Expose your horse to as many different things as you can think of to encourage his trust and keep him interested.

Try not to develop the habit of jumping with your horse as you may have great difficulty in keeping up with him should you ever compete in a jumper class with multiple jumpoffs. Also, it looks more professional if you don't jump with him. This is a class for your horse, not you. I will never forget seeing a gentleman at Nationals flying over the jumps with his horse—only, HE was the one that knocked the rail down and disqualified them both. If you have a horse that will not jump, let him follow a trained horse over a few low jumps to encourage him. Always remember to knot the end of your lead rope so that your horse doesn't continue the course without you.

Construct your jumps to meet the rule book specifications. Should you ever decide to compete, you and your horse will have the benefit of schooling over the proper sizes. *Never, ever* pull back or down on a horse that is just about to take off over a jump. You will completely throw off his natural timing and he will most likely refuse the jump or try to run out on it. Only with practice will your horse learn to judge the height and depth of each jump. Set up different courses so that your horse learns to turn both toward you and away from you during a jump pattern. If the horse knocks a few down, lower the jumps and try again the next day.

Measure your successes one jump at a time and don't take more than a few each day. Gradually build up his jumping ability. Be positive and encouraging on each and every jump. Do not scream, hit the horse, raise your voice or throw things at him to get him over the fence. Remember to always instill courage and confidence in him.

DRIVING COMPETITIONS

Driving a Miniature is every bit as exciting as driving a larger sized horse. There is a terrific sense of freedom and a very special interaction.

You can drive country roads, obstacle courses and dressage patterns, or show him off in parades and marathons, or simply make a trip to your mailbox.

At AMHA shows, Miniatures may be driven for pleasure at the walk, collected trot, and working trot while attached to two- or four-wheel carts as a single, pair, tandem, unicorn, four-in-hand hitch, or more. In obstacle driving classes, your Mini may be requested to back straight, drive over bridges, through water, mazes, zigzags, serpentines, figure eights, cloverleafs, or narrow passages. Variation in presentation is not uncommon in this class. The Mini can be spotted zooming by with a roadster cart, the driver with bright silks ablaze, or hitched to an elegant 4-wheel formal Viceroy cart, or hitched as a working team to a 4-wheel wagon. I have a picture of the Domino's Pizza wagon being pulled by a team of Miniatures, each named after a pizza topping.

All the elements of driving a Miniature Horse are the same as for driving their larger breed cousins. The American Driving Society is your best reference for equipment, safety, rules, and a good guide to other drivers and instructors in your area.

A word of caution: although the Miniature Horse is smaller in size, they can do just as much damage to themselves, you and your equipment as a large horse. The most important thing in maneuvering your horse in harness is that he must learn to stop dead in his tracks at any time you ask. His obedience could prevent a potential collision, allow you to avoid a hazard with your wheels, get your reins untangled from any other piece of your harness or the horse's tail, or simply to adjust your harness. Always have someone to head your horse as you hitch, unhitch, and get in and out of the cart. And *never, ever* remove the bridle for any reason while any part of the harness or cart is still hitched to the horse.

Driving classes at Miniature Horse shows are a pleasure to watch.

Always end your sessions on a good note with lots of pats and praise. That way he will be happy to see you the next time you come around to play.

*American Miniature Horse Registry approved shows also have these classes.

Training & Showing Miniature Horses 115

Raising A Well-mannered Foal
by Katie Schubert

When you're raising a foal, you must have an objective in your mind. Do you want a well mannered, docile, calm and accepting horse at the end of all your work? Or do you want a show halter horse with a little (or a lot) of spunk? Many people use different programs based on different ideas to achieve their goals, and what follows is a combination of methods used for training a young horse. The gentle nature of Miniature Horses makes handling and teaching Mini foals that much easier.

Starting early.

We talked to a couple of small breeders of fine, show-quality horses who wanted their stock to be well mannered: in one case, respectful and not too cuddly, and in the other case friendly, interested, and personable. The basic theme of both breeders is to catch them while they're young and impressionable.

Both of the breeders do all of their own preliminary training and then either send their two- or three-year-olds off to a professional trainer and sell them later as finished show horses. Or they sell their young stock as two- or three-year-olds, sometimes started in harness and with show potential to the buyer who wants to be involved with their new horse's early training and show career.

DAYS 1, 2 & 3

Both breeders agreed that during this period, the foal should be handled a little bit—touched, spoken to, and nearby when the mare is tended to and visited—but not too much. This is the time when bonding between mare and foal occurs, and if the foal interacts too much with people, the bond may be confused or not as strong.

At this time, it is a good idea to get the foal used to its halter. Put it on, and let the foal wear it for a while, supervised of course. Then put it on and take it off a few times.

FIRST TIME OUT

Most people take the mare and foal outside to a safe paddock on the third day. This gives the foal time to get his legs and strength up.

Both breeders agreed that it is a good idea to halter and lead both mare and foal. Some people don't bother with the foal, as he will automatically follow his mother anyway, but he will grow bolder daily, and stray a little on the way to the paddock. In many cases, leading the foal may be necessary from the very start for his safety, because of the distance to his paddock, or perhaps clutter or equipment in barnyard areas where horses would never be loose and an inquisitive foal would be in danger.

The fact that the foal will follow his mother is a definite advantage to you, as you don't really have to lead the foal. By the time it does become necessary, it will have become a habit with him, and he will most likely acquiesce without argument.

Finally, once you have started haltering the foal before he leaves his paddock or stall, never allow him to run loose or refuse to be caught. Once indulged, he won't forget, and will constantly take advantage of it. Even if it takes twenty minutes to catch the foal, invest the time or you may be sorry later. He will learn soon enough that he doesn't get to go anywhere until he stands still for a moment while you put his halter on.

NEXT FEW MONTHS

On a general guideline of weaning at six months, the next three should see you working with the foal in the confines of his stall with mom right there. Later on, work in the paddock, too, sometimes with, and sometimes without a halter.

At first, start each session by putting the mare's halter on, brushing her, and picking her feet up and cleaning them out. By this time the foal will be curious and interested in what you're doing, and when its his turn, he'll be glad to have the attention. Try to get in a few strokes with the brush, though he probably won't go in for a thorough grooming at first. Picking up his feet won't be very popular with him in the beginning either, so go at his pace, persisting only until he does it right once on each foot. "Doing it right" will start with a very low height, getting higher with time. After awhile, he should be willing to hold his foot up long enough for you to clean it, whether it needs it or not. Even though

Miniature Horse foals are tiny enough to "muscle around" when you need to do something like trim hooves, a well-mannered horse will learn to stand quietly while these chores are performed. It is up to you to teach him this.

Brush or play with his tail a little, too, to get him used to you standing behind him. He'll probably want to turn around to see what you're doing, so just follow his tail until he stops chasing you, again improving the standard with time. Handle and brush his face and ears so he gets used to the feeling and doesn't become head shy.

Finally, work with him on actively leading, with *you* in charge, in the stall or paddock. A butt rope may be helpful in propelling him forward at first. Make sure that with each tug on the butt rope, you also tug lightly on the lead rope. Never jerk the foal's head, as he will learn to resist when he feels the pressure. After a while you won't need the butt rope, returning to it over the next year only when he needs a reminder.

Walk him around, making him stay at your speed and go where you say, and make sure he stops when you want to, always accompanied by the word *"whoa."* Use it often and make sure he always obeys.

FOUR MONTHS—THE SEPARATION

Again, this is only a guideline, but for a couple of months before weaning, you should start to separate the mare and foal for gradually longer periods—this will make weaning easier.

At first, just take the foal out (it may be necessary to have someone hold the mare) and walk him around. Stay in sight of the mare in the beginning until the hysteria stops or lessens, and then go for longer walks, maybe handgrazing him a little.

Both our breeders agreed that its not a good idea to leave the foal alone in the stall, as he may hurt himself or try to climb out.

After a while, start to work on the same things as before: brushing, petting, picking up feet, etc. and maybe a little work with clippers. Get the foal used to the sound and vibration, and later the feel of actual clipping. Always go at the foal's pace and try to keep him from ever being frightened or hurt.

AFTER WEANING

Weaning should be relatively easy as a result of the separation periods, so you can usually continue immediately with his training. The next step is to teach the foal to tie or cross-tie. This stage requires your full attention, as a securely-tied foal that panics can break his neck or injure himself by falling. The principles of teaching to tie and cross-tie are the same, but we'll talk specifically about cross-tying. Remember to leave the lead rope on the foal at all times up until he is about a year old, maybe longer, depending upon the foal's stability. It's a familiar feeling and, if the foal panics, will help calm him, along with the now familiar word *"whoa"* and your familiar, soothing voice.

First, get the foal used to the idea of seeing ropes going from both sides of his head to the wall. Just loop the wall end of the rope around—don't tie it yet. Next, tie the ropes loosely to the wall using a quick-release knot, and make sure that the ropes are long enough, not putting tension on his head.

Don't do anything new around the foal that may frighten him when he is tied—keep doing all of the old familiar things like brushing him, picking up his feet, etc. While you're working around him, stop every few minutes and re-position him in the cross-ties, if necessary. Make sure he doesn't get too far back or forward and don't let him get sideways at all. Talk to him frequently, too. The sound of your voice will keep him calm. Remember, you are the one he looks to for guidance, and if he detects fear or panic in your voice or manner, he'll only panic more. It's up to you to stay calm in all situations.

Finally, for at least 4 months, do not leave the foal tied alone or get out of his sight and, even then, for only a few seconds at first, talking to the foal the whole time. Using comforting words, *"whoa,"* and repeating his name will keep his mind on you and *"where are you?"* rather than anything else going on, or the fact that he is alone.

If you are raising your Miniature Horses to be broodmares or breeding stallions, there are additional areas of familiarity that need to be established.

Training & Showing Miniature Horses

Start getting your fillies used to being touched around the insides of their back legs and the area where the udder will develop. They will probably be ticklish and squirm a lot, but continue to familiarize them with the feel of your hands. As they mature, they will tolerate being cleaned in this area and, when the time comes for foaling, this will make things easier (see *"Predicting Foaling,"* pg. 63).

For stallions at stud, cleanliness is of paramount importance at breeding time. If you begin early with your stud colts, cleaning the sheath and penis will be a normal grooming procedure that will not upset them. Start gradually, just handling the sheath and penis, and gently wiping it with a soft damp cloth or sponge. The purpose at this time is not cleanliness, but familiarity. You'll appreciate it later!

DISCIPLINE

During the first few months when the foal is building a relationship with you and you're gaining his trust, discipline should consist of no more than firm discouragement of unwanted behavior. You can achieve this with a loud, firm *"No!"* and make him cease whatever he's doing. If it is really bad, (e.g., he kicks you while you are brushing him) a sharp smack on the rump or shoulder along with a *"No"* should do the trick. Biting should be handled with a sharp rap on the sensitive muzzle. You'll probably have to repeat it a few different times before he gets the picture, so be patient. If the foal seems to revel in attention and company, walk away and leave him alone for a few minutes.

Over the next few months, the foal will develop a sense of what he should and should not do, and you'll be able to tell if he's just being naughty. NEVER let him get away with anything—dish out the customary smack, *"No,"* and always punish according to the crime. Raising your voice (not screaming) is also useful, as the horse will be upset by your loud voice, and will be able to sense your "anger" and displeasure with him. On the other hand, always reward him with pats and scratches, nice words like *"good boy"* or *"good girl,"* and use his name in friendly tones.

FOR LIFE OR LONGER

As gentle and good-natured as Miniature Horses are, lack of training and discipline can still result in aggressive "horse" behavior that is not acceptable. During all of his early training, think of what you want your grown horse to do, and how you want him to behave. Work on the basics

Good behavior has it's rewards!

from the very beginning, and by the time you get there, he'll be just the way you want him to be. All of this handling, and his growing comfort with you, will have instilled trust in you and people generally, which will make further training much easier. Go slowly and try to see things from his point of view, and you'll most likely always receive acceptance, even if hesitant at first, rather than fear and rejection of new things.

Reprinted from Eastern Miniature, July 1991.

SECTION 7
Tools of the Trade: Your Tack & Equipment

Buying Used Vehicles:
How to Tell a Plum from a Lemon
by Bonnie Kreitler

Used carriages, like used cars, come without much of a warranty. A used driving vehicle doesn't have so much as an odometer to tell you how much mileage it's already seen. You have to judge the amount of wear and tear for yourself and decide whether the vehicle is still sound enough to use or could be restored to usable condition. Whether you've just stumbled across what you hope is a bargain at an auction, answered a tempting classified ad, or heard of a vehicle via the grapevine, "let the buyer beware" prevails.

A pair of 33" Miniature Horse mares pulling a custom-built Bronson wagon.

KICKING TIRES

Alvin Raber, who builds and restores vehicles at his A & D Buggy Shop in Millersburg, Ohio, recommends that you start your examination of a used vehicle with the wheels. The first thing is to make sure that the wheels belong to the vehicle you are buying. Stories abound of people who have bought a vehicle with the wheels standing next to it, only to find out later that the two never went together in the first place. Wheelwright Bruce Tompkins, who is proprietor of the George E. Daniels Wagon Factory in Rowley, Massachusetts, suggests that buyers next look for any wood rot. A fingernail or the tip of a sharp penknife can be used to carefully probe any suspicious area to see if it is soft. Check the hub and the spokes and the *felloes*—the sections that make up the wheel's wooden perimeter. Tompkins also advises that you search for tiny holes about the size of a pinhead. They mean that Powder Post Beetles have been chewing away at the interior of the wood. The tiny holes are deceptive. The greater part of the damage is invisible inside the wood where the beetles have chewed their way along the grain of the wood, severely weakening it. This, says Tompkins, is the biggest problem with old wheels. Inspect the wheel for cracks or splits that make it unsound and potentially dangerous.

If the wheels themselves seem sound, check to see if they are loose on their axles by rolling the vehicle and watching for any side-to-side wobble. You can also grasp the rim and try to wiggle the wheel on its hub. A wheel that's just slightly loose may only need a new leather washer. Push the wheel all the way on, then try again to wiggle it sideways. If the wheel still moves, it probably means that there is wear and tear on the axle and hub that new washers alone won't remedy. Tompkins also recommends that buyers check the slight dish that any wheel shows from its hub out toward its rim. An exaggerated dish means that the wheel is getting old and as this dish becomes more pronounced, the wheel loses some of its strength. A loose spoke is not of particular concern as long as its hole in the hub has not become enlarged. Tompkins notes that if a wheel is used when the spokes are loose, the holes in the hub become elongated and the wheel goes downhill quickly. He cautions buyers to beware of wheels that have had loose spokes tightened by soaking the wheel in water. This is treating the symptoms instead of the cause, he says, and is dangerous. When all of the spokes in a wheel are loose, he likes to replace the *spider*—the hub and spokes—to restore the wheel to sound using condition.

When it comes to wheel repairs, buyers can use the rule of thumb that the farther out from the hub, the easier and cheaper the repair. Putting on a new rubber tire or a new channel that holds the tire is a relatively easy repair. If the wheels need to be replaced completely, older-style wheels with wooden hubs start at about $150, while a more modern wheel with a roller bearing hub will start at about $100. The size of the hub and the weight of the spokes determine the price more than the actual size of the wheel.

LOOKING FOR MOISTURE DAMAGE

Check the wood throughout the carriage for evidence of rot, beetle damage, or cracks as thoroughly as you checked each wheel. Check under floormats or seat cushions, if possible, and other areas such as corners and joints where moisture could have been trapped. Straight shafts that are cracked or warped by improper storage are easy to replace, costing $120 to $150 a pair, depending on their length. Shafts with a bent heel or curved tip run more. As with wheels, make sure that a removable pole or set of shafts really fits the vehicle you are considering. Leather trim and keepers on the shafts and singletrees are easily replaced if worn or dry-rotted.

Moisture adversely affects metal as well as wood, so rust is the next thing you should check. Raber feels that if a vehicle is more than 20 or 30 years old, it should be disassembled to look at the condition of its bolts and metal fittings. His shop holds many examples of bolts that looked sound from the outside, but hidden within the wood, were eaten away by rust at their middles. He counsels that, unless an older vehicle being restored is completely disassembled, you can never get at all of the rust. The rust builds up (between the leaves of the springs, for example) and will eventually work its way out and loosen any finish that's put on the metal.

WIRE WHEELS & CONSTRUCTION QUALITY

Many beginners start out driving lightweight wire-wheeled jogcarts with pneumatic tires. Carriage and harness dealer Phil Stanton of Wild As The Wind Farm in Upton, Massachusetts, advises Miniature drivers to watch out for the homemade variety. Unless their maker was skilled, Stanton says, they are often too heavy, poorly balanced, and have sharp angles in the metalwork that can hurt a horse. Stanton notes that wire-wheeled vehicles were originally developed for racing and then adapted for ringwork on a flat, consistent surface. They often have a narrower track width than a wooden-wheeled vehicle for the same-sized animal. This, coupled with their bouncy pneumatic tires, can make them very tippy when driven over rougher ground outside a ring.

A Miniature Horse being driven to a wire-wheeled jogcart.

Rubber is subject to rot, especially when tires are left standing for long periods of time on damp surfaces. Check the entire circumference. The condition of the tread and chrome plating on the wheels will give you some indication of how carefully the vehicle has been maintained.

Mary Lightner encourages buyers to check the overall construction quality of any vehicle they are considering. The hallmark of a good vehicle, she feels, is that it shows care with detail. *"If you see square butt ends and saw marks in the wood, or if the metal bracing has been sheared off without smoothing it, then you are looking at poor workmanship."* A good quality vehicle will show a smooth sanding job and the corners of wooden parts will be rounded and shaped. Look at the metal channel that holds the rubber tire and at the tire itself. These should be one piece, Lightner says—not pieced together out of several small strips. Spokes should sit squarely in the felloes. The leaves of the springs should line up and be well-seated on one another. If they are misaligned, they will shift in use.

If the vehicle you're looking at is a natural wood vehicle (that doesn't mean bare wood—it means that the wood has been protected with a clear finish such as varnish, rather than paint), it's easy to make the recommended examinations. However, if the vehicle has been painted, your job is a little harder. A classified ad in the local paper may lead you to a well-meaning, but misguided soul who took several cans of black spray paint to Grandpa's old runabout before offering it for sale. Or, at an auction, you may run into a just-restored buggy with a million-dollar look, only to find after you've taken it home that the paint peels in no time. Someone did a "quickie job" and didn't prime the wood properly. Worse yet, after the paint peels away, you might find a lot of wood filler hiding wood rot. Raber strongly counsels against buying completely restored carriage unless you know the reputation of the person who did the restoration.

FITTING AND BALANCING

Whether you're buying a new or used vehicle, you need to make sure that it fits the driver as well as the horse.

Stanton notes that when builders scale down a vehicle for a Miniature Horse, they sometimes don't leave enough leg room for the driver. The proportion of the seat height, boot and shaft must fit both man and beast. *"You want to show the animal off, without engulfing it by either a cart or a person,"* he comments. One good way of making sure that the vehicle fits you is to ask for a "test ride." While this isn't always possible, it can't hurt to inquire. Be sure that the seat is wide enough to hold two adults comfortably if you plan to take a companion driving.

Phil Stanton (right) demonstrates how a well-built horse cart should balance with weight in it. Your Mini cart should do the same.

At a minimum, check the balance of any two-wheeled cart you're considering. While you hold the shafts, put the number of people the vehicle will carry into it and slowly move the shafts up and down. In a well-balanced cart, the shafts will have a "weightless" feel at the point of balance. If this point is very far above horizontal, the cart will have a tendency to "lift" the horse. If you can't find any balance point, the horse will be carrying the weight of the vehicle and its occupants entirely on his backpad. A used cart may be for sale because its poor design gave someone else's horse a sore back!

Alvin Raber advises that if a bargain-priced vehicle will need a great deal of time and money to restore it, it may not be a bargain at all, and some vehicles may be unsafe to use without extensive repairs. *"There's enough danger to driving that you must know what you're getting into,"* Lightner admonishes beginners looking for their first equipment. Plan a few "browsing" expeditions to sharpen your detective skills and arm yourself with as much information as possible. Then, when you put money in your pockets, your buying trip should be a success.

Reprinted from Eastern Miniature, March 1991.

APPENDIX

Additional Reading

Books

Miniature Horses
by Dorothy Hinshaw Patent
1991; 48 pages, color, juvenile/adult
Published by Cobblehill Books, NY

Horse of the Future
by Jill Swedlow Coffey
1989; 106 pages, black & white, adult
Published by Glastonbury Press, CA

First Halter
by Kendrick Taylor
1994; 18 pages, black & white/color, adult
Published by Kendrick Taylor
Rt. 1, Box 125
Clifton Forge, VA 24422

A Horse for Everyone
by American Miniature Horse Assn.
1994; 24 pages, color, general info.
Published by AMHA
Alvarado, TX

Historical Sketchbook of Miniature Horses
by Jan Garbero
1987; 48 page coloring book, juvenile
Published by Jan Garbero
PO Box 83644
Phoenix, AZ 85071

Also see Bibliography, page 12.

Magazines/Newspapers

The Miniature Horse "Voice"
Monthly magazine
Subscription only
Published by Chris Carbone
PO Box 271
N. Pembroke, MA 02358

The Miniature Horse World
Bimonthly magazine
Subscription only
Published by AMHA, Alvarado, TX

The Journal
Bimonthly magazine
Subscription only
Published by AMHR
PO Box 887
Warrenville, IL 60555

Miniature Horse Marketsheet
Monthly tabloid
Free (postage only)
Published by Tom Cavin
PO Box 167457
Irving, TX 75016-7457

Miniature Horse News
Monthly tabloid
Subscription only
Published by Mary Jane Berry
PO Box 1384
Tomball, TX 77377-1384

Important Contacts

American Miniature Horse Assn.
5601 South I H 35W
Alvarado, TX 76009
817-783-5600 • Fax 817-783-6403

American Driving Society
PO Box 160
Metamora, MI 48455-0160
810-664-8666 • Fax 810-664-2405

American Miniature Horse Registry
6748 Frostwood Pkwy
Peoria, IL 61615
309-691-9671 • Fax 309-691-9687

American Horse Council
1700 K Street, NW, Ste. 300
Washington, D.C. 20006-3805
202-296-4031 • Fax 202-296-1970

ABOUT THE CONTRIBUTING AUTHORS

Maggie Anderson-Murphy is an attorney specializing in insurance and liability, practicing in Connecticut. She has been involved with horses all her life. She has written several articles for eastern horse publications.

Michael Berluti is a farrier in East Haddam, Connecticut. He has written several articles concerning foot care for *Eastern Miniature* magazine

Cindy Fisher is an equine author living in the Eastern Townships of Quebec.

Ted Garman has spent his life around horses and has been a trainer for several full-size breeds. He has trained and shown Miniature Horses for the past 7 years, with consistent success. He has given several driving clinics, sharing his trainer's wisdom and tips with Miniature Horse owners in the mid-Atlantic states. He resides in Lynchburg, Virginia.

Bonnie Kreitler is a well-known equine journalist. Her work has been published in most popular publications and she has won many awards for both her writing and photography. She works and lives in Fairfield, Connecticut.

Susan Larkin is a pedigree research specialist living in Wellington, Nevada.

Cheryl A. Lekstrom has been a horsewoman since 1968. She owns and runs Windcrest Acres, a Miniature Horse breeding farm in West Boylston, Massachusetts. She has spent her time promoting Miniature Horses through her writing, presentations, clinics, and open barn programs. She has contributed to many well-known equine periodicals over the years, sharing her wisdom and trainer's expertise with Miniature Horse owners everywhere.

Toni M. Leland has spent the last 15 years as a graphic designer and author, all within the horse industry. She has published two equine magazines during her career, as well as many annuals and periodicals. She has been writing educational articles for the horse industry since 1985.

Dr. Kenneth L. Marcella is an equine practitioner, journalist, professor, and lecturer. His practice is at the Equine Medical Center in Suwanee, Georgia. An English and Biology double major at Dartmouth college, he proceeded on to New York State college of Veterinary Medicine at Cornell University to obtain his graduate degree. Dr. Marcella has produced regular articles for many equine publications including *The Journal of the American Veterinary Association* and *Equine Practice*. He also consults for Cargill Feed company, answering management-related questions regarding nutrition and horse care.

Katie Schubert has spent her life with horses. She has ridden and shown her Morgans and Arabians, and has specialized in raising and training young foals. She has studied journalism and has written several articles for equine magazines. She lives and works in Haddam, Connecticut.

CREDITS

Except where photo credit is given, photographs were furnished by Equine Graphics. Illustrations, except as credited, are courtesy of Equine Graphics.

"Perilous Pasture Plants," by Cindy Fisher was reprinted with permission from Rural Heritage, spring 1995; publisher Allan Damerow, 281 Dean Ridge Ln, Gainesboro, TN 38562

"Pedigree and Breeding Terminology," by Susan Larkin was reprinted with permission from Southwestern Horseman, March 1995; publisher Southwestern Horseman, Inc., PO Box 40428, Eugene, OR 97404

AMHA STANDARD OF PERFECTION
As provided by AMHA (8/95)

General: A small, sound, well-balanced horse possessing the correct conformation characteristics required of most breeds—refinement and femininity in the mare and boldness and masculinity in the stallion. The general impression should be one of symmetry, strength, agility, and alertness. Since the breed objective is the smallest possible perfect horse, preference in judging shall be given the smaller horse, other characteristics being approximately equal. **Size:** Must measure not more than 34 inches at the withers, at the last hairs of the mane. **Head:** In proportion to length of neck and body. Broad forehead with large prominent eyes, set widely apart. Comparatively short distance between eyes and muzzle. Profile straight or slightly concave below the eyes. Large nostrils and clean, refined muzzle. Even bite. **Ears:** Medium in size. Pointed and carried alertly, with tips curving slightly inward. **Throat-latch:** Clean and well-defined, allowing ample flexion at the poll. **Neck:** Flexible, lengthy, in proportion to the body and type, and blending smoothly into the withers. **Shoulders:** Long, sloping and well-angulated, allowing a free-swinging stride and alert head/neck carriage. Well-muscled forearm. **Body:** Well-muscled with ample bone and substance. Balanced and well-proportioned. Short backs and loins in relation to length of underline. Smooth and generally level top-line. Deep girth and flank. Trim barrel. **Hindquarters:** Long, well-muscled hip, thigh, and gaskin. Highest point of croup to be same height was withers. Tail set neither excessively high or low, but smoothly rounding off rump. **Legs:** Set straight and parallel when viewed from front or back. Straight, true, and squarely-set when viewed from the side, with hooves pointing directly ahead. Pasterns sloping about 45 degrees and blending smoothly with no change of angle, from the hooves to the ground. Hooves to be round and compact, trimmed as short as practicable for an unshod horse. Smooth, fluid gait in motion. **Color:** Any color or marking pattern and any eye color is equally acceptable. The hair should be lustrous and silky. **Show Disqualification:** Height in excess of 34 inches. Monorchidsim* in Senior Stallions. Any unsoundness or inheritable deformity. If in doubt, the show judge may request the opinion of the show veterinarian. Non-disfiguring blemishes not associated with unsoundness or injuries which are temporary should not be penalized unless they impair the general appearance and/or action of the horse.

* having one testicle.

AMHR STANDARD OF PERFECTION
(as provided by AMHR 6/95)

A. General Impression: A small, sound, well-balanced horse. It should give the impression of strength, agility, and alertness. The disposition should be eager and friendly, not skittish.

B. Size: *Division A*—The American Miniature Horse must measure not more than 34 inches at the base of the last hair on the mane. *Division B*—The American Miniature Horse must measure not more than 38 inches at the base of the last hair on the mane.

Since the breed objective is the smallest possible perfect horse, preference in judging shall be given to the smallest, all other factors being equal. Priority in judging shall be in this order:
1. Soundness
2. Balance and conformity to the Standard of Perfection
3. Size

C. Head: In proportion to the body, neither excessively long or short. The eyes should be large, alert, and prominent with no discrimination for color. The ears should open toward the front and be carried erect. The teeth should show no signs of parrot mouth or undershot.

D. Neck: Strong and muscular, proportionate to body and type of horse represented.

E. Body: Well-muscled with good bone and substance; well-sprung ribs; level topline, as nearly as possible of equal height in withers and rump; fore and hindquarters well-angulated, so that the horse in movement shows a smooth gait.

F. Legs: Straight, clean and sound.

G. Hooves: Round and compact, trimmed as short as practical for an unshod horse and in good condition.

H. Color: Any color, eye color, and/or marking pattern is equally acceptable.

I. Throatlatch: Clean and well-defined, allowing ample flexion at the poll.

J. Shoulder: Long, sloping, and well-angulated, allowing a free swinging stride and alert head/neck carriage. Well-muscled forearm.

K. Hindquarters: Long, well-muscled hip, thigh, and gaskin. Highest point of croup to be the same height as withers. Tail set neither excessively high or low, but smoothly rounding off rump.

L. Disqualification: Height in excess of 34 inches for Division A and 38 inches for Division B Miniatures. Dwarfism, blindness, unsoundness, and cryptorchidism* in aged stallions.

*undescended testicles

GLOSSARY

allergic—hypersensitive to a specific substance.

anemia—a condition in which there is a reduction of the number of red blood corpuscles or of the total amount of hemoglobin in the blood resulting in lack of vigor or vitality.

ankylosed—fused joints or fibrous parts

antibodies—a protein produced in the body in response to contact with an antigen, with the specific capacity of neutralizing the antigen and creating immunity.

artificial insemination—a procedure where semen is placed in the mare's vagina by a veterinarian; the stallion never physically breeds the mare.

body brush—medium-stiff bristled brush used for removing dust & hair.

bonding—the crucial relationship development between mare and foal.

Brachygnathism—a deformity known as "parrot mouth" in which the upper jaw protrudes out farther than the lower jaw.

broodmare—a mare kept solely for breeding purposes.

cavaletti—a series of small wooden jumps used in the basic training of a horse to encourage it to lengthen its stride, improve balance, and strengthen muscles.

cervix—the opening of the uterus.

cesarean section—a surgical procedure where a foal is delivered through an abdominal incision in the mare.

chestnut—a horny growth on the inner side of a horse's legs, just above the knee in front and below the hock in back.

chromosomes—bodies within the cell nucleus that are composed of DNA and carry genetic information.

colic—sharp abdominal pain, often a symptom of gas or an obstruction created by food or feces; can lead to a twisted bowel and death.

colt—a young male horse under 2 years old.

colostrum—the first milk given by a mammal. Mare's colostrum contains important antibodies which are absorbed by the foal within 24-36 hours after birth.

concave—hollow and curved.

conceive—become pregnant

concussion—shock from impact

conformation—structure of the horse's body

convulsions—a violent, involuntary contraction or spasm of the muscles.

Corpus Luteum—a yellow body in the ovary that secretes progesterone, an important reproductive hormone.

cryptorchidism—failure of one or both testicles to descend to the scrotum after birth; testes may be retained within the abdominal cavity or inguinal canal.

culling—the elimination of undesirable animals from a breeding herd.

curry comb—grooming equipment used to remove dirt and scurf from a horse's coat; has a flat back with the front containing several rows of rubber or metal teeth.

dam—the mother of a horse.

debilitation—weakness

dehydration—loss of water from the body.

depressive—having the ability to depress.

deviation—anything other than the norm or standard.

diestrus—the period of a mare's estrous cycle when she will not accept a stallion.

dilation—being expanded or wider.

disproportionate—not in proportion.

dominant—overpowering or overriding.

dystocia—difficult delivery or birth

embryo—an organism during the earliest stages of development.

encephalomalacia—cerebral softening, usually a result of cutting off of the blood supply

encephalomyelitis—inflammation of the brain and spinal cord.

enzyme—a protein capable of accerlerating or producing change in another substance without itself being changed.

equine influenza—an acute, infectious, contagious viral disease, characterized by inflammation of the respiratory tract, fever, and muscular pain.

equine—a horse; of or pertaining to horses.

erratic—not consistent or regular.

estradiol—the female sex hormone.

estrous cycle—the complete reproductive cycle of the mare.

estrus—the time during a mare's cycle when she is in "heat" or "season" and will accept a stallion.

farrier—blacksmith, horseshoer.

feces—manure.

fertile—reproductively healthy.

fetotomy—a surgical procedure where a dead fetus is cut to facilitate removal from the mare.

fetus—an unborn organism during the later stages of growth and development.

filly—a young female horse under two years of age.

float—remove the sharp edges from a horse's teeth.

foal—a baby horse.

Follicle Stimulating Hormone—the female hormone that stimulates the production of a follicle in the ovary.

follicles—the cell that encases and nourishes the egg as it develops within the ovary.

forage—food for domestic animals, fodder.

frog—the triangular horny pad in the sole of a horse's foot.

gastrointestinal—relating to the stomach and intestines.

gelding—a castrated male horse.
genes—the determiner of hereditary traits; a segment of a DNA molecule.
genetics—dealing with heredity or variation in similar or related animals and plants.
genotypes—the gene type that an individual inherits from both parents.
gestation—the growth and development period of the fetus inside the womb; in the horse, it is approximately 11 months.
get—the offspring of a stallion.
Gonadatropin Releasing Hormone—the hormone that travels to the ovaries and stimulates the Follicle Stimulating Hormone.
grooming—cleaning and brushing.
hand-breeding—a mating where the mare and stallion are controlled by handlers, rather than being allowed to breed at will.
heritability estimate—the term for assessing the probability that a trait will be passed from parents to offspring.
hoof pick—a device for cleaning out the underside of the hoof, around the frog.
Human Chorionic Gonadatropin—a human hormone that helps induce ovulation in the mare when given at the right time.
hybrid vigor—when two individuals are crossed and the resulting offspring is superior to either parent.
hydrocephalus—water in the brain cavity where brain tissue should be.
hypersensitivity—excessively sensitive
hypothalmus—a part of the brain that regulates many body functions.
immune system—that which controls an organism's susceptibility to disease.
immunologic—pertaining to the immune system.
inbreeding—the mating of closely-related individuals or of individuals having similar genotypes.
induced—artificially started.
infertility—reproductively inactive or nonproductive.
insemination—introduction of semen into the vagina.
laminitis—inflammation of the laminae in the horse's foot, with resulting lameness.
linebreeding—a conservative program of inbreeding designed to concentrate the blood of a certain ancestors within the linebred offspring.
listlessness—having no interest in what is going on.
luteal tissue—matter that fills the ruptured follicle after the egg has been released.
Luteinizing Hormone—hormone produced by the pituitary that stimulates the development of corpora lutea in the mare.
lyse—degenerate
malformations—abnormal formations.

malleable—workable, pliable.
malocclusion—teeth do not fit properly together to grind food.
mare—an adult female horse.
maternal—on the mother's side.
meiosis—cell division
monorchidism—complete absence of one or both testicles.
mucous membrane—a membrane that secretes mucus.
muzzle—the area just below the nose.
nausea—sensation of feeling like vomiting.
nicking—crossing well with certain individuals.
open—not in foal.
orofacial—having to do with the mouth and face.
outcrossing—breeding two individuals who have no common ancestors for 5 generations or more.
ovaries—two gonads in the mare that contain germinal cells.
ovulation—the release of the egg from the ovary.
ovum—egg
paddock—fenced area for keeping a horse.
palpation—manual inspection of internal organs.
parturition—delivery or birth.
paternal—on the father's side.
pedigree—the ancestral "family tree"
penis—the male reproductive organ.
photosensitive—sensitive to light
physiology—the functions and vital processes of living organisms.
pigment—coloring matter in cells and tissues.
pineal gland—part of the horse's brain that senses the amount of daylight through a nervous system connection with the eyes.
pituitary gland—secretes hormones influencing growth and metabolism.
placenta—a vascular organ that surrounds the fetus during gestation and connected to it by the umbilical cord; the fetus receives nourishment and excretes waste matter via this organ.
polyestrus—a mare that cycles throughout the year.
producer—term used for a productive mare.
progenitor—term used for a productive stallion.
progeny—offspring of either mare or stallion.
progesterone—hormone produced by the corpus luteum which quiets uterine muscle contractions.
Prognathism—mouth abnormality known as monkey mouth, where lower jaw sticks out farther then upper jaw.
Prostaglandin F2alpha—the hormone generated by the uterus that affects the corpus luteum and causes it to degenerate.
recessive—not dominant
resorbed—absorbed
respiratory—relating to the lungs and chest.

Rhinopneumonitis—a highly-contagious disease causing abortion in pregnant mares or mild upper respiratory infection in young horses.
roaching—shaving the mane completely down to the neck
roughage—hay, grass; needed by horses for proper digestion.
run-in shed—usually 3-sided shed, open at the front; used for shelter.
scratches—a painful condition of the lower legs caused by mud and hair that is constantly wet.
selection—the process of upgrading a herd of animals.
sheath—the protective covering of the penis in the male horse.
short cycle—to bring a mare back to receptivity sooner than the 21 days standard; this is done by administering a timed dose of PGF2a
siblings—brothers and sisters
sire—father
sound—healthy and usable.
stagnant—standing water that has become brackish and sour.
stall vices—bad habits acquired by horses that become bored standing in a stall all day and night.
stallion—an adult male horse capable of producing offspring.
stifle—the knee-like joint above the hock on the hind leg of a horse.
strangles—an infectious and highly contagious disease, occurring most commonly in young horses; high temperature, thick nasal discharge, swelling of lymphatic glands of the head, which eventually abscess.
suffocation—death from lack of oxygen.
tack—the equipment such as halter and harness used for training or using a horse.
temporomandibular joint—the jaw hinge.
tendon—a fibrous cord of connective tissue that attaches muscle to bone or other structures.
Tetanus—an infectious, often fatal disease caused by a micro-organism living in the soil; usually enters the body through wounds, especially of the foot.
thrush—inflammation of the frog of the foot, characterized by a foul-smelling discharge; caused by unclean, damp bedding or pasture and lack of proper hoof cleaning.
topline—the outline of the horse from the poll to the croup.
toxicosis—poisoning
traction—adhesive friction used for movement, as of the horse's foot on the ground.
trait—a distinguishing quality or characteristic.
trauma—bodily injury, wound, or shock.
tremors—trembling of the limbs, caused by muscle spasm.
udder—the mammary gland of the mare; also called the "bag."

ultrasound—ultrasonic waves used in diagnosis or pregnancy detection; sound waves at a very high frequency bounce against the fetus and then back to the monitor, forming a picture on the screen.
unthriftiness—poor condition.
urinary incontinence—the condition of being unable to control urination.
uterus—womb; the reproductive organ where an embryo/fetus develops.
vulva—the external genitalia in the mare.
waxing—term used to describe the small drops of waxy material that form on the ends of the nipples very close to foaling time.
weaning—separating a mare and foal, so the foal cannot nurse its dam; usually done at 4-6 months of age.
weanling—a young horse of either sex under the age of 1 year.
whorl—an area on the haircoat where the hairs grow in a spiral or coil; can be used for identification similar to fingerprint whorls.
windsucking—also known as cribbing; a vice usually acquired due to boredom, but becoming a habit; the horse grabs the edge of the stall door or fence, pulls back and gulps air.
winging—an improper way of going where the front feet "wing" out to the sides as the horse trots.
yearling—a horse between the ages of 1 and 2 years.

Watch for our *complete* equine dictionary

Coming Soon!

SMALL HORSE PRESS
a division of Equine Graphics Publishing

Small Horse Press
ORDER FORM

The Miniature Horse in Review, Vol. 1. The only Miniature Horse Resource Book of its kind! Basic ownership, health issues, breeding and raising Minis, legal and insurance concerns, buying and selling Minis, training and showing your horses, and purchase and care of equipment and tack. All articles written by equine professionals. 136 pages plus lots of photos and illustrations—$23.95 ppd.
Order #MRV1.   *Publication date: 10-1-95*

Getting Started With Minis Series. Four books packed with the necessary information that every new Mini owner needs and wants. Written by equine professionals specifically for new owners. Available separately or as a set. 24-32 pages with plenty of illustrations and photographs. Part 1: The Basics (32 pgs)—$9.95 ppd. **Order #GS1;** Part 2: Miniature Horse Health (24 pgs)—$7.95 ppd. **Order #GS2;** Part 3: Training & Showing (24 pgs)—$7.95 ppd. **Order #GS3;** Part 4: First Time Breeder (32 pgs)—$9.95 ppd. **Order #GS4;** All four books—$29.95 ppd. **Order #GSA.**   *Publication date: 9-1-95*

Breeder's New Owner Gift Pack. Put the finishing touches on the sale of your Minis! Regular gift pack includes beautiful 8-1/2x11 pedigree form on parchment, suitable for framing, 2-sided complete horse health record form, New Owner's Basic Checklist, Barn First-Aid Kit List, Registry contact information, List of Miniature Horse magazines, order form for Small Horse Press publications, and a special gift from us. Just fill out the pedigree form and enclose your business card and farm brochure or information in the packet. Makes customers remember you when they are ready for another Mini!—$5.95 ppd. **Order #BGPR.**
Custom packets are available with the pedigree imprinted with your logo and farm name and the horse's information filled out in fine calligraphic script.—$9.95 ppd. (One-time set up fee of $15.00) **Order #BGPC.**   *Publication date: 9-1-95*

Name _____ Phone _____

PO Box _____ Club Aff? _____

Street Address _____

City _____ State _____ Zip _____

Send check/m.o. to
Equine Graphics Publishing
537 Drager Street
Ashland, OR 97520.
Sorry, no C.O.D/ credit cards

**RUSH?
Of Course!**
Just Call for Details
541-488-8135

What information or products would YOU like to see? Call us— We're Open To Suggestions!

QTY	ORDER #	PRICE	TOTAL
	MRV1	$23.95 ppd	
	GS1	9.95 ppd	
	GS2	7.95 ppd	
	GS3	7.95 ppd	
	GS4	9.95 ppd	
	GSA	29.95 ppd	
	BGPR	5.95 ppd	
	BGPC	9.95 ppd	
	BGPC Set-up	15.00	
		Total Enclosed	

Here's a Sneak Preview of What You'll Find in
Volume Two
The Miniature Horse in Review

- *Getting your Mini's feet ready for show season*
  - *Driving tips for amateurs*
    - *Alternative veterinary medicine*
  - *Preparing to talk to your banker*
- *Respiratory disease in the Miniature Horse*
  - *Managing a breeding stallion*
    - *Taking care of those precious foals*
  - *Proper record-keeping*
    - *Training your own Miniature*
      - • • *And much, much more...!*

Publication date: Spring 1996

SMALL HORSE PRESS
a division of Equine Graphics Publishing